Keep it simple and strong

Contemporary Survival English

Maximize your English with idioms, spoken expressions and in-depth reading.

prof. Moon, young soo/ Cheon, jae yun

BAEKSAN
Publishing Co

Preface

2011년 봄이다. 지천에 벚꽃이 흐드러지게 피어있는 모습을 보니 어느새 감상에 젖어든 자신을 발견하게 된다. 이러한 자연의 아름다움에도 불구하고 대학교와 어학원에서 학생들을 지도하다보면 다음과 같은 생각이 든다.

"어떻게 하면 영어 실력을 향상시킬 수 있을까?"

이러한 물음에 대한 답으로 그간 여러 권의 책을 집필할 수가 있었다.

이번에 출판하는 Contemporary Survival English는 이디엄, 기본회화, 구어체회화, 독해기법, 독해로 구성되어 있다. 책명처럼 동시대를 살아가려면 이 정도 수준은 알아야 할 거라는 생각으로 집필을 시작했다.

끝으로, 집필과정에서 영감을 주신 하나님께 모든 영광을 드리며, 앞으로도 "내 뜻이 아닌 그분의 뜻" 으로 살아가길 소망하는 바이다.

2011년 아름다운 봄날

저자 문영수 · 천재윤

Contents

Ⅳ. Fast Reading skill 87

Ⅴ. Various English Reading 121

I

Essential English Idiom

I Essential English Idiom

1 come into the limelight(=spotlight) 각광을 받다

If someone **comes into the limelight**, a lot of attention is being paid, because they are famous or because they have done something very unusual.

- He came into the limelight after he finished it.

2 split with 갈라서다, 의견이 다르다

If you **split** it, it is divided into two or more parts.

- I have to split hairs with you.
- How could he split up with her?

3 twist one's arm 비유적 표현으로 강요하다

If you **twist someone's arm**, you persuade them to do something.

- She is not twisting your arm.
- He had twisted her arm to get her to do it.

4 hit / strike home

마음에 와 닿다, 정곡을 찌르다

If a situation or what someone says **hit home or strike home**, people accept that it is real or true, even though it may be painful for them to realize.

상대방으로부터 반응을 얻을 때 쓰는 표현이다.

- My face was pale as her words hit home.
- Did the reality of the situation hit home?

5 have butterflies in one's stomach

두근거리다

If you **have butterflies in your stomach**, you are very nervous about something.

- An interview or exam may produce butterflies in the stomach.

6 Achilles heel

약점, 급소

the weak spot in a man's circumstances or character

To attack **the heel of Achilles** means that he or she has the weakest point in something.

- This may be the Achilles heels of the plans.
- She does have an Achilles heel.

7 Your nose is growing. 거짓말 마렴, 안속아

You're lying to me. That's a lie. 의 뜻이다.

- I won't fall for your tricks. Your nose is growing.
- Your are not honest for the money. Your nose is growing.
- Be honest! Your nose is growing.

8 be warm 가까워지다

퀴즈나 게임에서 정답에 가까워질 때 쓸 수 있는 재미있는 표현이다. 반대말은 be cold로 '멀어지다'의 뜻이다.

- His guess is getting warmer.
- You're getting colder.

9 ring a bell 생각이 나다

If you say that something **rings a bell**, you mean that it reminds you of something, but you cannot remember exactly what it is.

- It doesn't ring a bell.
- His name doesn't ring a bell.

10 vanish into thin air 감쪽같이 사라지다

thin air은 無를 나타낸다.

- It seems to vanish into thin air.
- Money vanishes into thin air.
- My car had vanished into thin air.

11 fill to the brim 가득 채우다

brim '그릇의 가장자리' If something **is filled to the brim or full to the brim** with something, it is filled right up to the top.

12 be in the same boat 같은 처지이다

If two or more people **are in the same boat**, they are in the same unpleasant situation.

- We are all in the same boat.
- We are all in the same boat on this.
- Everybody is in the same boat.

13 make no bones about

개의치 않다, 인정하다

If you **make no bones about** doing something that is unpleasant or difficult or that might upset someone else, you do it without hesitating.

- I had no bones about reapplying for the test.
- He made no bones about telling her what he thought of her.
- I make no bones about it.

14 long shot

가망 없는 일

If you describe something as a **long shot**, you mean that it is unlikely to succeed.

- Your team was a long shot to win the final game.
- It's a long shot, but it just might work.
- It's going to be a long shot.

15 on the house

공짜로, 무료로

If you are given something in a restaurant or shop **on the house**, you don't need to pay for it.

- It's on the house. = It's on me.

- Drink up. It's on the house.
- Everything is on the house tonight. Don't worry about it.

16 keep one's head above water 간신히 살아가다, 빚지지 않다

- She is keeping her head above water.
- I couldn't keep my head above water.
- He is doing his best to keep his head above water.

17 fish or cut bait 태도를 분명히 하다, 거취를 분명히 하다

양자 간에 태도를 분명히 하라는 뜻으로 상대방의 단호한 결단을 촉구할 때 사용할 수 있다.

- It's time to either fish or cut bait.
- Quit wasting time! Fish or cut bait!
- There's been enough discussion. It's time for us to fish or cut bait.

18 No sweat 별거 아냐, 문제 없어

걱정할 일도 아니고 어려울 것도 없고 문제될 것도 없음을 나타낼 때 쓸 수 있는 표현이다.

- No sweet without sweat.

❀ Thanks for your advice. Hey, no sweat!

19 wise guy

잘난체 하는 사람, 분수도 모르는 사람

비격식 표현으로 부정적 의미로 쓸 수 있다.

If you say that someone is a **wise guy**, you dislike the fact that they think they are very clever and always have an answer for everything.

❀ Mind your own affairs, wise guy.

20 Bottoms up!

건배, Cheers의 의미

참고로 formal한 표현으로는 **I would like to propose a toast to~** 가 있다.

❀ Bottoms up for our success!

❀ I would like to propose a toast to the greatest mother that ever lived.

21 to cap it all

결국에 가서, 설상가상으로, 최악의 것은

안 좋은 일이 지속적으로 일어나다가 최악으로 어떤 일이 발생한 경우에 사용한다.

❀ To cap it all, he lost his job.

- To cap it all, he spent all his fortune.
- To cap it all, the tsunami happened after the earthquake.

22 cut corners 절차를 무시하다, 경비를 줄이다

If you **cut corners**, you do something quickly by doing it in a less thoroughly way than you should.

- When money is short, it is necessary to cut corners.
- Profits from cutting corners may be vast.
- Cut corners with the paper work.
- I can't cut corners just because everyone does.

23 weather the storm 어려움을 견디다, 난국을 돌파하다

If someone **weathers the storm**, they succeed in reaching the end of a very difficult period without much harm or damage.

- He insists he will not give up the plan and will weather the storm.
- Remember how well we weathered the storm after the recession.
- I believed my son would weather the storm.

24 turn the corner　　고비를 넘기다, 모퉁이를 돌다

어려운 상황을 벗어난 경우 사용한다.

- We're hopeful we've turned the corner now.
- She watches him turn the corner to the trauma hallway.
- Unfortunately, she never seems to turn the corner.
- I feel I've turned the corner.

25 It takes two to tango.　　손바닥도 마주쳐야 소리가 난다

If you say it **takes two to tango**, you mean that a situation or argument involves two people and they are both therefore responsible for it.

상황에 따라 긍정적으로, 부정적으로 사용할 수 있다.

- They are separated. It takes two to tango.

26 land someone in hot water　　곤경에 처하게 하다

hot water 곤경

- This sort of behaviour will land her in hot water.
- Occasionally your mouth lands you in hot water.
- She may be in hot water over lying about it.

27 bad news 일차적 의미로 나쁜 소식, 이차적 의미로 일상적으로 불쾌감을 일으키는 사람이나 일 모두에 적용함

- I have good news and bad news.
- The bad news made his blood boil.
- Be prepared for some bad news.

28 hit the books 열심히 공부하다

hit은 study보다 informal한 표현이다.

- Our exams are soon so we had better start hitting the books.
- Hit the books if you want to succeed in your life.
- She has got to hit the books.
- Stop complaining about it and hit the books.

29 pipe dream 헛된 꿈, 망상, 공상

pipe이란 단어를 통해 꽉 채워진 상태가 아니라 비어있는 상태임을 알 수 있다.

A **pipe dream** is a hope that will never come true and happen.

- It was just a pipe dream.
- She realized that it was a pipe dream.

❀ It is something of a pipe dream.

30 give weight ~을 중요시하다, 관록을 붙이다

weight이란 단어에서 알 수 있듯이 어떤 일에 중요성을 부과하는 경우이다.

❀ How about giving more weight about it?

❀ We should give weight to the statement.

❀ He gave special weight to the matter.

31 burn oneself out = overtax 사력을 다하다, 무리를 하다

지속적인 일로 기진맥진했을 때 사용하는 표현이다.

❀ She'll burn herself out. She needs to take a break.

❀ There's no need to overtax her strength.

❀ She had overtaxed her energies lately.

32 What's the occasion? 무슨 날이야?

상대방이 평소와는 다른 옷차림을 할 때나 초대를 받을 때 사용할 수 있다.

❀ A : Let's get together tonight.

B : What's the occasion?

33 no matter what

누가 뭐래도, 무슨 일이 있어도

어떠한 일이 있어도 무언가를 해내겠다는 것을 의미하는 표현이다.

- No matter what happens, you must survive.
- No matter what happens, he keeps his composure.
- No matter what he does, he's always complaining.

34 You name it.

말해보세요, 무엇이든지, 모두 다 있다

You say **you name it** to indicate that you are talking about a very wide range of things.

- You name it. Anywhere is okay with me.
- You name it. I have done it.
- You name it. I'll try.

35 broke

한 푼도 없는, 무일푼의

If someone is **broke**, he or she has no money.

- I'm as broke as he is.
- I'm afraid I am broke.
- She's broke, but she doesn't need your help.

36 go out of business
회사가 문을 닫다

반대말은 **be in business, be open for business.**이다.

- Business as usual.
- The store went out of business three years ago.
- After 7 years in business, we're going out of business.

37 the bottom line
결론, 문제의 핵심

가장 기본이 되면서도 핵심적인 것을 나타낼 때 사용한다.

The bottom line in a decision or situation is the most important factor that you have to consider.

- The bottom line is it's a complicated situation.
- The bottom line is that the economic situation do not improve.
- Look, here is the bottom line.

38 limbo
망각, 중간상태, 미결상태

limbo란 천국과 지옥의 중간상태로 예수 이전에 태어난 착한 사람 또는 세례를 받지 않은 어린이의 영혼이 머무르는 장소이다.

- Official permission was in limbo.
- The case was in limbo.
- We are in a kind of limbo.

II

Everyday English Conversation

II Everyday English Conversation

1 인사 표현

일상적인 만남에서

A : What's up?

B : Nothing much. How about dinner tonight?

A : Would 7:20 be okay?

B : Good! I'll see you then.

Note Nothing much와 같은 표현으로는 Not much가 있다.

A : How did the test go?

B : Terrible, I don't even want to talk about it.

Note Terrible은 Awful, Miserable의 뜻이다.

가족 안부 묻기

A : How have your family been?

B : They have been doing well.

오랜만에 만났을 때

A : Do you remember me?

B : Oh, my God, Jae-yun. How have you been?

A : I'm doing fine, thanks. How about your parents?

B : They've been doing well.

A : Long time no see! How have you been?

B : Great, I miss you.

A : Wow, you sure have changed!

B : It's been 7 years already! Time flies.

Note 오랜만에 만나는 경우

I haven't seen you lately.
How have you been?
Who set you free?
What have you been up to?

소개로 만났을 때

A : It's nice to meet you. I have heard a lot about you.

B : All good I hope! Pleasure meeting you too.

A : I don't believe I got your name.

B : Oh, my name is Jae-Yun Cheon. Nice to meet you.

Note 기타 소개표현

I feel like I know you already.
Dr. Moon talks about you often.
Excuse me, Could I get your name, please?
Could you tell me more about yourself?
Here's my business card.
We grew up together.

헤어질 때

A : See you again soon.

B : Yes, I've had a good time.

A : Take care!

A : Same time next week?

B : Okay, see you then.

A : It's time I got going

B : I think I've taken up too much of your time.

Note It's time I got going.

= *It's time for me to go.*
It (가주어/형식주어/예비주어) *for me* (*to*부정사의 의미상 주어) *to go* (진주어)

기타 헤어질 때 사용 표현

So long.

It was nice meeting you.

Keep in touch.

Catch you later.

I'd better get going.

See you around.

Well, see you again.

Time to head back to the office.

I'd like to see you once more.

We'll have to do this more often.

Have a nice weekend.

Sounds good. I'll see you then.

Have a safe trip home.

2 관광 표현

예약하기(reservation)

A : United Airlines. Susan, speaking. May I help you?

B : Yes, I'd like to make a reservation to Hawaii on Aug 4, Sunday.

A : Thank you. I can make a reservation for you on Flight 303 which leaves 10:20 a.m.

B : All right. I will take it.

A : What class would you like economy, business or first?

B : Business class.

A : Your name and phone number, please?

B : Jae-yun Cheon, 010-4634-3840.

A : How do you spell?

B : J-A-E-Y-U-N, C-H-E-O-N.

A : Thank you, your reservation is made for Flight 303 leaving for Hawaii on Aug 4, 10:20 a.m. You'll have to reconfirm your reservation at least three days before your departure.

B : Thank you. Bye.

예약 취소(cancelling)

A : United Airlines. Susan, speaking. May I help you?

B : I want to cancel my reservation for the flight from Seoul to Hawaii on Sunday.

A : Your name, please?

B : Jae-Yun Cheon.

A : All right. Your reservation is cancelled.

B : Thank you.

탑승 수속(check-in)

A : Good afternoon. What can I do for you?

P : I want to check in, please.

A : May I see your ticket and passport, please?

P : Here it is.

A : How many baggages do you have?

P : Just two.

A : Here are your boarding pass and baggage claim check. Enjoy your trip.

P : Thank you.

호텔 투숙

A : I'd like to check in.

B : Do you have a reservation?

A : No.

B : You need a reservation, sir.

A : Do you have any vacancies?

B : I'm afraid not.

A : Okay.

안전한 여행에 대한 소망

A : I just want to get there in one piece.

B : Don't worry.

호텔에서 체크아웃 할 때

A : I need to check out.

B : All right, sir.

A : Do you accept BC card?

B : We take cash only.

A : Are you serious?

관광지에서 사진 찍기

A : Would you mind taking our picture?

B : O.K. Smile.

A : May I take a picture with you?

B : O.K.

기타 관광 관련 표현

What do you think I should see here?

What's the admission fee?

How do I get there?

Do you have any brochures?

Would you mind taking me around?

I could show you around.

It's on the way.

Come along.

Could you recommend a good restaurant?

How much do the tour cost?

Where can I buy a bus pass?

3 전화 표현

전화벨이 울릴 때

A : The phone's ringing. Is someone going to get that?

B : I'll get it. It's for me.

누구를 찾는지?

A : Who do you want to talk to?

B : Mr. Cheon, please.

A : He just stepped out.

B : Can I leave a message?

A : Sure.

지금은 없다

A : She's not here at the moment.

B : Do you know when she'll be back?

A : She'll be back by 3:00.

전화 바꿔 주기

A : Could you put me through to Mr. Cheon?

B : He's busy. Would you call again please?

Note 기타표현

I'll transfer you.
I'll connect you with him.
I'll switch you over to him.

자리에 없을 때

Prof. Cheon is not here at the moment.

He is tied up right now.

He hasn't come in yet.

I'm afraid Mr. Cheon is no longer with us.

He's out for lunch.

전화가 왔는지 물어보는 표현

Did anyone call me?

Why did she call?

전화 받기가 곤란한 경우

A : She can't really talk right now.

B : OK, I'll call her back in just a few minutes.

Note **기타 표현**

Make it short. I don't have much time
Get to the point
It's not a good time.
I'm in the middle of dinner.
Call me back in a little bit?

상대방이 잘못 전화를 건 경우

A : You've got the wrong number. We don't have anyone by that name.

B : I'm really sorry.

잘 듣고 있는지 확인하기

A : Are you listening to me?

B : I didn't catch that last part. Could you speak more slowly?

잘 안 들리는 경우

Could you call me back?

Are you there?

What's that noise?

Can't you hear it?

I'm sorry but I'm having a problem with my phone.

Your phone is dead.

전화를 끊을 때

I guess I've got to go.

Thanks for calling.

I'll have to get off the line now.

전화기를 오래 붙들고 있는 경우

The telephone is her best friend.

Don't make love to the phone.

Aren't you off the phone yet?

Don't be on the phone.

She's been on all day.

4 의견 묻기

상대방 의견 물어 볼 때

A : How do you like going to America this summer?

B : That would be nice.

A : I need your two cents on something. *two cents : 의견, 견해

B : I am sorry, but I don't know what to do.

A : What makes you say that?

B : Let me give my opinion. I'm totally against it.

상대방 의견에 찬성

You said it.

I agree with you.

We speak each other's language.

You sold me.

You're telling me.

You're a genius.

That's it.

I'll go along with that.

상대방 의견에 반대

I don't agree with you.

You didn't understand anything.

I'm afraid you've missed the point.

I think you're mistaken.

결심하기

She has made up her mind.

It's final. There's nothing more to discuss.

I'm telling you like it is.

That's absolutely right.

5 상점에서

옷가게에서

A : Can I help you, sir?

B : I need to have this wrapped.

A : What wrapping paper do you prefer?

B : How about that one?

A : Good choice. And the ribbon?

B : Oh, blue, of course!

꽃가게에서

A : May I help you?

B : I'd love to buy some flowers.

A : For what occasion, ma'am?

B : They are for two sons, Yu-Beom, Hui-Beom.

A : Are you thinking of cut flowers?

B : Yes. Can you deliver for me?

A : Of course.

약국에서

A : I have a splitting headache. I can't do anything.

B : We have some aspirins.

A : I'll take it, then.

6 화재시

A : Oh, No! Look! There's a fire.

B : Let's call the fire department.

A : We want to report a fire.......

B : We'll send the fire engine right away.

7 놀이공원에서

A : Cotton candy! Dad, let's go!

B : Stay close beside me.

III

Useful American Expression

Ⅲ Useful American Expression

A bit annoying, really.	정말로 귀찮을 지경이었지.
A little help would be good.	조금만 도와주세요.
Absolutely not.	절대 아닙니다.
Act your age.	철 좀 들어라.
Action will be taken soon.	조치가 곧 취해질 겁니다.
Admit it.	인정해.
All you have to do is ask.	부탁만 하세요.
Allow me.	내가 할게.
And what?	그래서?(재촉할 때)
Any comments?	의견 있나요?
Anytime will be fine.	언제든 좋아요.
Are there many people ahead of me?	제 앞에 사람이 많나요?
Are we allowed to take pictures in here?	여기에서 사진을 찍어도 될까요?
Are you close for lunch?	점심때 닫나요?
Are you decent?	들어가도 되니?
Are you in much pain?	많이 아프나요?
Are you sure about that?	그것에 대해 확실하니?
Are you trying to rip me off?	바가지를 씌우려고요?

Are you two close?	둘 사이는 좋아?
As good as can be expected.	더 이상 바랄 수 없을 정도죠.
Be my guest.	편한 대로 하세요.
Be nice.	좀 잘해줘라.
Because of you, I'm in a bad mood.	너 때문에 기분이 나빠.
Believe me.	나를 믿어.
Better late than not.	안하는 것보다 하는 것이 낫다.
Better now?	이제 나아졌니?
Bite your tongue!	말조심해.
Both sides refuse to fold.	양측이 팽팽히 맞서 있다.
Bummer.	안됐구나.
Business is business.	공과 사는 구별해야지.
Call me tonight.	오늘 밤 전화해.
Can I bring you anything?	내가 준비할 거 있니?
Can I call you?	전화해도 좋으니?
Can I get on the subway around here?	이 근처에서 지하철을 탈 수 있나요?
Can I have the recipe?	요리법 좀 알려주세요?
Can I reserve a ticket over the phone?	전화로 표를 예약할 수 있습니까?
Can I tempt you?	한 잔 할래.
Can we get the bill?	계산서 좀 주실래요?
Can we have a table by the window?	창가 쪽으로 주실래요?
Can we move it up an hour?	한 시간 앞당길까요?
Can you be more specific?	좀 구체적으로 말해주실래요?
Can you come down a little on this?	깎아주실래요?
Can you give me an estimate?	견적 좀 내주세요.
Can you roll down your window?	창문 좀 열어줄래요?

Can you save my place in line?	자리 좀 지켜주실래요?
Can you send a taxi here immediately?	여기로 즉시 택시 좀 보내 주실 수 있습니까?
Can you send this to my office?	사무실로 보내실 수 있나요?
Catch the ball!	공 받아.
Catch you later.	이따 보자.
Clam up.	조용히 해.
Cold is better.	차가울수록 좋아.
Come here often?	여기 자주 오니?
Congratulations on your scholarship!	장학금 받은 거 축하합니다!
Could I speak with the manager, please?	당신의 상사와 얘기할 수 있나요? (음식점 등에서)
Could you page her for me?	그녀를 방송으로 불러주실 수 있나요?
Could you pull up here?	여기서 세워 주실래요?
Could you wrap this?	포장해 주실래요?
Could you write it down?	적어 주실래요?
Cut it out!	집어치워!
Cut this for me.	이것 좀 잘라줘요.
Describe what you see.	뭐가 보이는지 말해라.
Did I wake you up?	제가 깨웠나요?
Did you get all that?	다 적었나요?
Did you make your bed?	잠자리 정리했니?
Did you pass the class?	그 수업 패스했니?
Ditto.	나 역시.
Do I look like I am easy?	내가 만만하게 보여?
Do something.	어떻게 좀 해봐요.

Do we have everyone?	다 탔나요?
Do you go out of town?	시외로 가실 수 있나요?
Do you have a bus for pick-up and drop-off?	통학버스가 있나요?
Do you have a first-aid kit?	구급상자 있으세요?
Do you have a time?	시간 있으세요?
Do you have any brochures?	팸플릿 있나요?
Do you have any recommendations?	추천하실 만한 것이 있나요?
Do you have anything cheaper?	더 싼 것은 없나요?
Do you have change for a dollar?	잔돈 좀 바꿔주세요.
Do you leave the light on after bedtime?	잘 때 불을 켜 놓나요?
Do you live on or off campus?	학교 안에서 사나요, 아님 밖에서 사나요?
Do you see any parking spaces?	주차할 공간 있어요?
Do you take cream in your coffee?	프림 넣으세요?
Do you think people will notice?	사람들이 알아 챌 거라고 생각하니?
Do you want to drive? No? Then shut up.	네가 운전할래? 안 할 거면 가만히 있어.
Do you want to grab a bite?	뭐 좀 먹을까?
Does it work?	효과 있어요?
Don't be pushy.	강요하지 마.
Don't beat around the bush!	빙빙 돌리지 말고 핵심을 말해.
Don't beat the air.	헛수고 하지 마.
Don't change the subject.	말꼬리 돌리지 마세요.
Don't cut it too short.	너무 짧게 자르지 마세요.
Don't get technical.	어려운 말마라.

Don't give it that.	말도 안되는 소리 하지 마.
Don't go too far.	너무 오버하지 마.
Don't go woolgathering.	헛수고 마.
Don't hit my nerve.	내 성질 건들지 마.
Don't I know you?	저를 모르세요?
Don't jump to conclusions.	섣불리 판단하지 마세요.
Don't keep me in suspense.	어서 이야기 해봐요.
Don't kill yourself over it.	그런 문제로 자신을 혹사시키지 마.
Don't leave anything out.	하나도 빠뜨리지 마세요.
Don't let it bother you.	그 일 신경쓰지 마.
Don't make it any worse than it is.	일을 더 악화시키지 마라.
Don't make love to the phone.	전화 좀 끊어.
Don't open up too fast.	쉽게 마음을 주지 마.
Don't order me around.	이래라 저래라 명령하지 마.
Don't rush me.	재촉하지 마.
Don't sit your hands.	빈둥거리지 마.
Don't take it out on me.	나한테 화내지 마렴.
Don't take it personally.	너 들으라고 한 소리가 아니야.
Don't talk to me like that.	듣기 싫어요.
Don't tell me about my world.	나의 세계에 대해서 말하지 마.
Don't try to drag me into this.	이 일에 끌어들이려 하지 마.
Don't you try to lie.	거짓말 하지 마.
Drop by if you're in the neighborhood.	근처에 오면 들르세요.
Enough already.	이미 충분해.
Enough is enough.	해도 너무 했다.
Every minute.	언제든

Everybody down.	모두 엎드려.
Everybody has a skeleton in his closet.	털어서 먼지 안 나는 사람 없어.
Everybody turn in your assignments at the end of class.	수업 후 과제를 제출해 주세요.
Everything I said came out wrong.	내 얘기가 모두 잘못 전해졌다.
Everything seems like a waste of time.	모든 게 시간 낭비인 것 같아.
Everything will turn out fine.	모든 게 좋아질 거야.
Everything's back to normal.	모든 게 정상화됐습니다.
Everything's gonna be okay.	다 잘 될 거에요.
Exactly what is that?	정확히 그게 뭐죠?
Excuse my appearance.	이런 꼴로 맞게 되어 미안해요.
Fair's fair.	좋은 것이 좋은 것이다.
Fill out the teacher evaluation form.	선생님 평가서를 작성해 주세요.
Fine. One more. Last one.	좋아. 하지만 마지막 하나 더.
Get a hair cut?	머리 좀 잘라.
Get a life!	정신 차려!
Get it off your chest.	속 시원히 털어놔 봐.
Get it?	알아들었니?
Get the ball rolling.	시작하렴.
Get with your partner.	파트너와 함께 하세요.
Give me a ring as soon as it's done.	끝나면 전화주세요.
Give me another opportunity.	한 번만 기회를 더 주세요.
Give me some feedback.	조언 좀 해주세요.
Give me the bottom line!	요점만 말해.
Give me time to realize my crime.	내 죄를 깨달을 시간을 줘요.
Glad to have you as part of the team.	당신이 우리 팀이 되어서 기쁘다.

Go in one ear and out the other.	한귀로 듣고 버려.
Go out and get some air.	나가서 바람 좀 쐐.
Go up to your room.	네 방으로 올라가렴.
Going my way?	저랑 같은 방향으로 가세요?
Good point.	좋은 지적이야.
Got a minute?	시간 있니?
Hand over my money.	내 돈 내놔.
Hang on a second.	잠깐 기다려.
Have a safe trip home.	무사히 가길 바래.
Have a sit.	앉으세요.
Have it your way.	좋을 대로 해.
Have we ever met before?	우리가 전에 만난 적 있나요?
Have you been drinking tonight?	오늘 밤 술 드셨나요?
Have you ever been on any medi-cation?	약을 복용한 적이 있나요?
Have you gone crazy?	당신 미친 거 아니요?
Have you got to be here all day?	하루 종일 여기 있어야 합니까?
He acts very mature for his age.	그는 나이에 비해 성숙해.
He cuts me in the street.	그는 나를 모르는 척 해.
He got an academic scholar-ship.	그 사람은 성적 장학금 받았어.
He got canned.	그는 해고됐어.
He has poor social skills.	그는 사교성이 없어.
He is a baby face.	그는 동안이다.
He is a member.	그는 평범해.
He is at the top of the tree.	그가 일인자야.
He is eating dirt.	그가 모욕을 참고 있어.

He is short of generosity.	그는 도량이 부족해.
He is talking down to me.	그는 나를 무시하며 말해.
He is under fire.	그는 비난받고 있어.
He looks so dejected.	그는 너무 풀이 죽어 보여.
He never listens to me.	내말을 안 들어.
He puts his foot in his mouth.	그는 함부로 말해.
He rings his own bell.	그는 자화자찬 해.
He was just here.	조금 전까지 있었어요.
He's a has-been.	그는 한 물 갔어.
He's always the center of attention.	그는 항상 이목을 받아.
He's cut out for the job.	그는 그 일에 적격이다.
He's direct in talking.	그는 직선적으로 말해.
He's got a heavy heart.	그는 무거운 심정이야.
He's got a one-track mind.	그는 융통성이 없다.
He's got more color.	혈색이 도는군요.
He's got no courage.	그는 용기가 없어.
He's no ordinary man.	그는 보통사람이 아니야.
He's not here at the moment.	지금 안 계십니다.
He's on the ball.	그는 재능이 있다. 머리가 좋아.
He's out at the moment.	그는 잠시 자리를 비웠다.
He's spoiled.	그는 버릇이 없어.
He's the type of person who loses his temper easily.	그는 쉽게 화를 내.
He's totally lost his cool.	그는 완전히 이성을 잃어버렸다.
He's turning in front of us.	우리 앞에서 방향을 바꾸고 있어요.
He's very bossy.	그는 권위적이다.

He's very disturbed.	정신적으로 불안정해요.
Here or to go?	여기서 드실 건가요, 아니면 가져가시나요?
Here's my best offer.	최선의 제안을 하나 하겠어요.
Hold your horses.	진정하세요.
How are you going to pay your tuition?	수업료 지불을 위해서 어떻게 할 겁니까?
How can I get in touch with you?	어떻게 연락하지?
How can I repay you?	어떻게 보답을 해야 할까요?
How can you be so sympathetic?	어떻게 그렇게 냉담할 수 있지?
How come?	어쩌다가? / 왜? / 어째서?
How could you treat me like this?	네가 나를 어떻게 이렇게 대할 수 있니?
How did that happen?	어쩌다가?
How did you do that?	어떻게 하셨어요?
How did you do this term?	이번 학기 성적 어때?
How do I call overseas?	국제전화는 어떻게 하죠?
How do I do this?	이것을 어떻게 하죠?
How do you think you did on the test?	시험 어떻게 본 것 같아?
How does Korea strike you?	한국의 첫인상이 어때요?
How late are you open?	몇 시까지 영업하나요?
How long has it been?	이게 얼마만이에요?
How long were you there?	거기에 얼마나 있었는데요?
How long will it take to develop the pictures?	사진 현상하는데 얼마나 걸리나요?
How many credits are you taking?	몇 학점을 수강하나요?
How many exposures are left?	필름이 몇 장 남았습니까?
How many people are you expecting?	몇 명 정도 올 것 같나요?

How many stops away is it?	몇 정거장 떨어졌죠?
How many times do I have to tell you?	내가 도대체 몇 번 말했니?
How much did you put down?	계약금은 얼마 지불했죠?
How much is it all together?	전부해서 얼마죠?
How much is it for an oil change?	엔진오일 교체하는데 얼마나 드나요?
How much longer will my order be?	주문한 것을 얼마나 더 기다려야죠?
How much longer will my order take?	주문한 것이 얼마나 더 걸리죠?
How often do you have to fill your car up?	얼마나 자주 주유하시나요?
How often do you work out?	운동은 얼마나 자주하죠?
How often does the bus stop here?	여기서 버스가 얼마나 자주 정차하나요?
How should I address you?	어떻게 부를까요?
How was it?	어떻게 그럴 수 있지?
How was your day?	오늘 하루 어땠어요?
How's business going?	사업이 어떻게 되어갑니까?
How's it going?	어떠세요?
I almost forgot your face.	네 얼굴 잊어버리겠다.
I am getting married.	나 결혼할거야.
I am pressed for time.	나는 시간에 쫓기고 있어.
I am sorry, that's all I know.	죄송하지만 그게 제가 아는 전부예요.
I apologize for the inconvenience.	불편하게 해드려서 죄송해요.
I blacked out.	필름이 끊겼다.
I can barely hear you.	잘 안 들려요.
I can't answer that at present.	현재는 대답할 수 없어요.
I can't believe you did this to me.	난 네가 나한테 이런 짓을 했다니 믿기가 어려워.
I can't come down anymore.	더 이상 할인은 안돼요.

I can't concentrate.	집중이 안 돼.
I can't eat another bite.	더 이상 못 먹어.
I can't get home.	집에 못 가겠어.
I can't get out.	빠져나갈 수 없어요.
I can't handle the heat.	더운 것은 못참어.
I can't let you go.	당신을 보낼 순 없어요.
I can't make ends meet.	형편이 어려워.
I can't pinpoint it.	꼭 집어 말하기 어려워.
I can't put a face to the name.	이름과 얼굴을 매치시키지 못하겠어.
I can't seem to shake this cold.	감기가 안 떨어져요.
I could be wrong.	내가 틀릴 수도 있죠.
I couldn't sleep a wink.	한숨도 못잤다.
I demand my payment.	대가를 지불하시오.
I did a double check.	두 번 검사했어.
I did them myself.	제가 직접 했어요.
I didn't get a bill from you yet.	청구서를 받지 못했어요.
I didn't get your homework.	학생의 과제를 못 받았어요.
I didn't know half the answers.	답을 절반 정도 모르겠더라고.
I didn't know where to get off.	어디서 내려야 하는지 몰랐다.
I didn't mean to do that.	결코 고의가 아니야.
I didn't quite hear you.	잘 듣지 못했어요.
I don't belong here.	난 여기 있을 수 없어.
I don't blame you.	널 비난하지 않아.
I don't care to hear more.	더 듣고 싶지 않소.
I don't care.	상관없어요.
I don't feel well about it.	나도 맘이 편하지 않아.

I don't have that kind of money.	많은 돈은 없어요.
I don't know my way around here.	잘 모릅니다.
I don't need your sympathy.	네 동정은 필요하지 않아.
I don't see anything I want.	원하는 게 없어요.
I don't see the end of this.	도대체 끝이 안 보이네.
I don't think I can.	힘들 것 같아요.
I don't think I'm going.	나는 안가는 게 좋을 것 같아.
I dreamed of you.	당신 꿈을 꿨어요.
I drink socially.	나는 사교상 술을 마셔.
I feel a big burden to do it.	그것을 하는 데 큰 부담을 느끼고 있다.
I feel disheartened to hear that.	듣고 보니 힘이 빠져.
I feel heavy.	몸이 찌뿌듯하다.
I feel it in my bones.	장담해.
I feel like a new person.	날아갈 것 같은 기분이야.
I feel like I know you already.	당신을 이미 알고 있는 것 같아요.
I feel like million.	기분 짱이다.
I feel tense lately.	최근에 긴장을 많이 해.
I feel the same.	동감입니다.
I forgot where I last had it.	어디다 두었는지 몰라요.
I get really nervous in public.	대중·앞에서 초조해요.
I get the picture.	알았어요.
I get worn-out easily.	쉽게 피로해요.
I got on the wrong side of the tracks.	제가 지하철을 반대편에서 잘못 탔어요.
I guess I'll be going.	아무래도 가야겠어.
I guess I've got to go.	끊어야 할 것 같아요.
I had mixed feelings about it.	기분이 교차했습니다.

I had my fortune told.	점 봤다.
I had to drop someone off.	누구 좀 내려줬어요.
I have a company coming.	일행이 있어요.
I have a lot on my plate.	할일이 많아.
I have a talent for making people feel comfortable.	나는 사람들을 편안하게 해주는 재주가 있어.
I have an early day tomorrow.	내일 일찍 일이니야해.
I have mixed feelings about it.	시원섭섭해요.
I have so many regrets.	나는 후회가 많이 남아.
I have some laundry.	빨래가 있어요.
I have ten minutes to kill.	10분을 때워야해.
I have to cancel.	취소할게요.
I have to slim down.	살을 빼야해.
I haven't had a bite since yesterday.	어제부터 굶었어.
I haven't seen you around in a while.	한동안 안 보이시던데요.
I hope I didn't offend you.	기분을 상하지 않았으면 해요.
I hope it's nothing serious.	심각한 게 아니길 바래요.
I just came one step ahead of you.	당신보다 조금 먼저 왔어요.
I just heard about him.	들어서 아는 사람이죠.
I know how you feel about it.	당신 기분을 알아.
I know how you feel.	심정 이해합니다.(장례식에서)
I know you're making this up.	너 지금 지어내고 있지.
I let you down.	너를 실망시켰어.
I live under my parent's roof.	부모님이랑 살아요.
I lost the whole file.	전체 파일이 날아갔어.
I messed up.	제가 다 망쳤어요.

I moonlight.	부업을 해.
I must know what it is.	난 그게 뭔지 알아야겠어.
I need a bit more time.	시간이 좀 더 필요해요.
I need a tow.	견인을 해주세요.
I need it back right away.	제가 지금 그것을 돌려받아야겠어요.
I need some cash.	현금이 필요해요.
I need to get a sleep.	잠 좀 자야 돼.
I need to get some shut-eye.	잠깐 눈 좀 붙여야겠어요.
I need to reschedule my flight.	스케줄을 조정하고 싶어요.(항공예약)
I need to take your blood pressure.	혈압 좀 재야겠습니다.
I never forget a face.	한 번 보면 기억해.
I never said that!	그런 말 한 적 없어.
I object!	나는 반대야!
I present you.	너에게 주는 거야.
I ran out of time and didn't get finished.	나는 시간에 쫓겨서 다 끝내지 못했어.
I really learned a lot in that class.	저는 그 수업에서 많은 것을 배웠습니다.
I seem to be lost.	길을 잃은 것 같아요.
I stayed up all night studying.	공부하느라 밤새웠어.
I think I got short-changed.	거스름돈을 덜 주신 것 같은데요.
I think I've taken up too much of your time.	제가 시간을 너무 많이 뺏은 것 같아요.
I think there's a leak somewhere.	어딘가에서 새요.
I think these people are leaving.	이 사람들 나가는 것 같아요.
I think you're taking the long way around.	당신 너무 돌아서 가는 것 같네요.
I totally lost my composure.	난 완전히 침착성을 잃었어.

I want to express my appreciation.	감사의 말을 전하고 싶어요.
I want to make a good impression.	좋은 인상을 주고 싶어.
I want to put in for a raise.	급여인상을 신청하려고요.
I want to sit sandwich.	가운데 앉을래.
I want you to take back what you just said.	방금 그 말 취소해.
I was able to just swerve around it.	차를 획 돌려 간신히 피할 수 있었어요.
I was at a loss what to say.	뭐라 해야 할지 몰랐어.
I was born and raised here.	전 이곳 토박이입니다.
I was born for this.	난 타고난 체질이야.
I was disconnected.	전화가 끊겼어.
I was here before.	전에 왔었는데요.(진료소)
I was hoping this would be a happy ending.	나는 이게 해피엔딩이길 바랬어.
I was humiliated.	창피했습니다.
I was sobering up.	그때 정신이 들었지.
I was talking to myself.	혼잣말이었어요.
I was tied up on the freeway.	교통체증에 묶여있어.
I was tongue tied.	말문이 막혔다.
I wasn't born yesterday.	난 애송이가 아냐.
I will have potential.	가능성이 있어.
I will turn in.	자야겠어.
I wish I could turn back the clock.	시간을 되돌릴 수만 있다면.
I won the lottery.	복권에 당첨됐습니다.
I work the night shift.	야간조 근무입니다.
I work the day shift.	주간조 근무입니다.

I'd like to check in.	체크인 하려고요.
I'd like to file a complaint.	항의를 제기하고 싶어요.
I'd like to make an appointment.	예약하려고요.(진료예약)
I'd like to schedule my vacation.	휴가 스케줄 잡고 싶어요.
I'll be busy all weekend.	주말 내내 바쁠 거야.
I'll be done soon.	곧 다해요.
I'll be free after 9.	9시 이후 괜찮아.
I'll be in the office all afternoon.	오후 내내 사무실에 있을 거야.
I'll check.	검사해 볼게.
I'll do whatever you want.	네가 원하는 어떤 것이라도 해주겠어.
I'll get you there in time.	제시간 안에 모셔다 드릴게요.
I'll give it a thorough checkup.	종합점검을 해드리죠.
I'll give you something that should help.	도움이 될만한 것을 줄게.
I'll go first.	제가 먼저 하죠.
I'll hang up and call again.	끊고 다시 걸죠.
I'll have the same.	같은 걸로 주세요.
I'll keep my eyes open for you.	눈여겨 볼거야.
I'll keep my fingers crossed.	행운을 빌어요.
I'll keep you in my prayers.	항상 기도해 드릴게요.
I'll never be hungry again.	다신 굶주리지 않을 거야.
I'll pay for this.	제가 지불할게요.
I'll take care of my business.	내 일은 내가 할 거야.
I'll take this one.	이걸로 살게요.
I'm a moderate drinker.	나는 술을 적당히 마십니다.
I'm all booked up today.	나 오늘 바빠.

I'm all in.	지쳤어.
I'm all set.	전 모두 준비했어요.
I'm all thumb.	잘못해요.
I'm all thumbs today.	오늘은 실수투성이다.
I'm behind in my work.	일이 밀렸어.
I'm burn out.	지쳤다.
I'm done for the day.	일과를 다 마쳤어요.
I'm dying to see you.	네가 몹시 보고 싶어.
I'm expecting company.	올 사람이 있어요.
I'm far too outspoken.	내가 지나치게 언성을 높였어.
I'm finished with it.	다 읽었어.
I'm finished.	드디어 해냈어.
I'm flying.	날아갈 듯해.
I'm glad you could make it.	와주셔서 감사해요.
I'm going back to bed.	좀 누워야겠어.
I'm having suicide feelings.	자살충동이 들어.
I'm heading in the same direction.	같은 방향입니다.
I'm just a little under the weather.	몸이 안 좋아요.
I'm just about to call you.	막 전화하려고 했어.
I'm just browsing.	그냥 둘러보고 있어요.
I'm just getting by.	가까스로 살아요.
I'm just going to be here for a few minutes.	몇 분 안에 돌아올 겁니다.
I'm not getting in the middle of this.	이 일에 끼고 싶지 않아.
I'm off tomorrow.	내일 쉬는 날입니다.
I'm on cloud nine.	매우 기뻐.

I'm on my way.	그곳으로 곧 갈게요.
I'm positive.	정말이야.
I'm really happy for you.	네가 잘돼서 기뻐.
I'm returning a call.	답신 전화입니다.
I'm running on empty.	기름이 텅 빈 채로 달리고 있어.
I'm sick and tired of it.	진짜 지겨워.
I'm so angry I could blow.	너무 화가 나서 터질 것 같아.
I'm so nervous my hands are sweaty.	너무 긴장해서 손이 다 젖었어.
I'm soaked through and through!	속옷까지 젖었어.
I'm speechless.	말문이 막힌다.
I'm starving.	배고파 죽을 지경이야.
I'm still working on it.	진행 중이죠.
I'm sure you would have done the same for me.	당신도 저한테 그렇게 해줬을 거예요.
I'm taking a bath.	망했다.
I'm taking a term off from school.	한 학기 휴학 중입니다.
I'm under a lot of pressure.	많이 시달리고 있어요.
I'm walking on air.	매우 기쁘다.
I'm with him.	그와 동행이다.
I'm worried about your son's progress.	아드님 진척 상태가 걱정이 되는군요.(학교생활)
I've got food poisoning.	식중독에 걸린 것 같아요.
I've had enough for today.	오늘은 이만 해야겠어요.
I've had enough.	많이 먹었어요.
I've seen everything.	별일 다 보는군.
Is anyone sitting here?	여기 자리 있나요?
Is financing available?	할부도 가능하나요?

Is it OK to park here?	여기에 주차해도 괜찮나요?
Is it too late to get a refund?	환불받으려고 하는데 늦었나요?
Is my car ready to go?	다 고쳤나요?(정비소에서)
Is there a bus stop around here?	이 근처에 버스정류장이 있나요?
Is there a cure?	치료법이 있나요?
Is there a good place to catch taxis near here?	이 근처에서 택시 잡기 좋은 곳이 있나요?
Is there a phone outlet in your room?	네 방에 전화 꽂는 데 있니?
Is this a transfer station?	여기가 환승역인가요?
Is this all you have?	이게 전부인가요?
Is this seat taken?	자리 있나요?
Is this your latest model?	최신 모델인가요?
Isn't that something?	놀랍지 않아?
Isn't there an easier way?	더 쉬운 방법은 없을까요?
It could be so exciting.	너무 재미있겠는걸.
It fits you well.	잘 어울려요.(의류에 관하여)
It has a lovely view.	경치 좋다.
It has a smooth ride.	승차감이 좋아요.
It hurts my conscience.	양심에 꺼려.
It hurts to talk.	말할 때 아파요.
It is nature.	그것은 본성이야.
It is not always perfect.	항상 완벽하지는 않아.
It is once in a lifetime chance.	평생 있을까 말까한 기회야.
It is our own choice.	그건 우리의 선택이야.
It just melts in your mouth.	입에서 살살 녹아.
It just slipped out.	그건 무심코 한 말이다.

It looks fake.	가짜 같아요.
It serves him right.	자업자득이지.
It slipped my mind.	깜박 잊었다.
It stopped.	그쳤어.
It takes two to tango.	손바닥도 마주쳐야 소리가 나.
It took me a while, but I finally realized.	시간이 걸리긴 했지만 깨달았다.
It was all my fault.	그건 모두 제 잘못이에요.
It was so embarrassing.	너무 당황스런 일이었어.
It was worth a try.	노력할 가치가 있었어.
It was wrong from the beginning.	기본부터 돼먹지 않았다.
It won't bite.	널 해치진 않을 거야.
It won't hurt to try.	해봐서 해될 것 없어.
It won't take long.	오래 걸리지 않을 거야.
It's a formal affair.	격식을 차린 모임이야.
It's a long short.	가능성이 희박해.
It's a natural thing.	그것은 자연스러운거야.
It's a pie in the sky.	그림의 떡이죠.
It's a pity she died so young.	젊어서 죽다니 안됐다.
It's a pretty short notice.	너무 갑작스런 부탁이지.
It's a real eyesore.	정말 꼴불견이야.
It's a sign of the times.	요즘 세상은 그래.
It's against store policy.	가게 규정에서 벗어나요.
It's all kind of technical.	내용이 너무 전문적이야.
It's around the corner.	머지않았어.
It's been a tough(long) day.	힘든 하루였어.

It's dead ahead.	막다른 길이야.
It's gonna be fun today!	오늘은 즐거운 하루가 될 것 같아.
It's happened before.	전에도 있었던 일이잖아.
It's in vogue now.	그건 현재 유행이죠.
It's just a pipe dream.	헛된 공상이야.
It's just one of those things.	어쩔 수 없는 일이잖아.
It's just talk.	괜히 하는 소리지.
It's just what I wanted.	그것은 바로 내가 원했던 것이다.
It's my turn to pay.	내가 살 차례야.
It's not your mistake.	너의 잘못이 아니야.
It's not your fault.	당신 잘못이 아니에요.
It's nothing. Let's go into the house.	아무 일도 아니야. 들어가자.
It's now or never!	지금 아니면 안 돼.
It's on the tip of my tongue.	입안에서 뱅뱅 도네.
It's so special to me.	그건 제게 각별합니다.
It's such a small thing.	사소한 것에 불과해.
It's the same thing over and over.	같은 일의 반복이군.
It's time for some new tires.	새 타이어로 교체할 때가 된 것 같습니다.
It's too late for that.	너무 늦었어요.
It's up to you.	너 하기에 달렸어.
It's using a lot more gas than usual.	평소보다 기름을 많이 먹어요.
Just a sec.	잠깐 기다리세요.
Just a touch.	조그만.
Just as you are.	단지 당신이기 때문에.
Just be yourself.	침착하세요.
Just buzz if you need anything.	필요하신 게 있으면 벨을 누르세요.

Just chicken feed.	쥐꼬리만큼.(월급이 적음을 나타냄)
Just do it.	한 번 해봐요.
Just in case.	만약을 대비해서.
Just lean on me when you need someone.	누군가 필요할 때는 그냥 내게 기대.
Just leave her alone.	그녀를 내버려둬.
Just let me know when you're finished.	끝나면 얘기해줘요.
Just my luck!	운이 없군.
Just promise one thing.	하나만 약속해줘.
Just the thought of it made me shudder.	그것만 생각하면 부들부들 떨려.
Keep away from me!	물러서요!
Keep it to yourself!	너만 알고 있어!
Keep it up!	계속 그렇게 해.
Keep pouring.	계속 따르세요.
Keep your complaint to yourself.	불평 좀 그만 해라.
Keep your shirt on.	기다리세요.
Keeping busy.	바쁘게 지냈어.
Kill the radio.	라디오 좀 꺼주세요.
Knock it off!	그만둬!
Let it all hang out.	만사를 잊고 쉬고 싶어.
Let me clarify that for you.	제가 명확히 설명하죠.
Let me get off here.	여기에서 내려 주세요.
Let me get that for you.	제가 가져다 드릴게요.
Let me pay for mine.	내 것은 내가 지불할게.
Let me sleep on it.	곰곰이 생각해 볼게요.
Let me write it down for you.	적어 드릴게요.

Let this be said.	모두에게 공표하겠다.
Let's catch a movie tomorrow.	내일 영화보자.
Let's face facts.	사실을 직시해.
Let's get going.	시작합시다.
Let's give him a big hand.	박수를 보내자.
Let's go bar hopping.	2차 갑시다.
Let's go by the book.	원칙 대로해.
Let's go for it.	해보자.
Let's hear your opinion.	당신 의견은 뭐예요.
Let's just forget about what happened.	과거 일은 잊자.
Let's let sleeping dogs lie.	긁어 부스럼 만들지 말자.
Let's make it a rush.	서두르자.
Let's pass the hat.	돈을 거두자.
Let's stop playing word games.	말장난 그만 하자.
Let's take this outside!	밖에서 한 번 붙자.
Let's talk over coffee.	커피마시며 얘기하죠.
Lie on your back.	드러누우세요.
Like what?	어떤 것?
Listen to your teacher.	선생님 말씀 잘 들어.
Listen we got a little problem.	들어봐, 우리에게 작은 문제가 생겼어.
Look who he is.	누가 왔나봐.
Lunch is on me.	점심 내가 살게.
Make sense anyway.	그럴 듯해요.
May I ask the nature of your business?	용건이 뭐죠?
May I get by?	좀 지나갈까요?
May I have a word in your ear?	귀 좀 빌릴까?

Maybe more than that.	그 이상일지도 모르지.
Might is right.	힘이 정의야.
Mistakes happen.	실수란 생기게 마련이야.
Money is no object.	돈은 문제가 안 돼.
My battery is dead.	배터리가 나갔어.
My chest feels heavy.	숨쉬기가 힘들어요.
My daughter won't stop crying.	딸이 계속 울어요.
My eyes are really itchy.	눈이 간지러워요.
My position is very uncomfortable.	내 입장이 난처해.
My vision is blurry.	시야가 흐려요.
Never say die.	죽는 소리 마.
Next time, come over to my house.	다음에 저희 집에 놀러오세요.
Nice talking to you.	얘기 즐거웠어요.
Nice talking with you.	대화 즐거웠습니다.
No big deal!	별거 아냐!
No hard feeling.	너무 언짢게 생각하지 마.
No need to apologize.	사과할 필요 없어.
No two ways about it.	두 말 하면 잔소리.
No way!	안 돼.
No, I can't take it.	안돼요. 전 받을 수 없어요.
Not much, same old.	별로, 늘 그래.
Not on your life.	말도 안 되는 소리.
Not that I know of.	전 몰라요.
Not this time.	지금은 좀 곤란해요.
Nothing like that.	그런 게 아니야.
Nothing's impossible.	불가능은 없어.

Now you're talking.	이제야 말이 통하는 구나.
Oh, you're here.	드디어 오셨군요.
Only for a while.	아주 잠시 동안만.
Only on special occasions.	특별한 날에만.
Our prices are fixed.	정찰제입니다.
Over my dead body.	내 눈에 흙이 들어갈 때까진 안 돼.
Pay your fare.	요금 내세요.
People like that really aggravate me.	저런 사람은 정말 날 화나게 해.
Period!	할 말 다했어!
Picture to yourself.	상상해보렴.
Please accept my deepest condolences.	깊은 조의를 표합니다.
Please accept my heartfelt apologies.	저의 진심어린 사과를 받아주십시오.
Please be careful when you exit.	나가실 때 조심하세요.
Please be more careful in the future!	다음엔 좀 더 신중해라!
Please describe your symptoms.	증상을 말해보세요.
Please drop me off here.	여기서 내려주세요.
Please get in.	어서 타세요.
Please make up my room.	방을 청소해 주세요.
Please put in a word for me.	잘 좀 얘기해 주세요.
Please, make it quick.	좀 빨리 가죠.
Pop quiz!	예고 없는 시험입니다.
Potential for what?	무슨 잠재력이요?
Pull over at the next area.	다음 휴게소에서 차를 세워.
Pull your own weight.	힘내렴.
Put a lid on it.	차를 세워.
Quit interfering.	상관하지 마.

Remember I'll get you back someday.	원수를 갚을 거야.
Ridiculous.	말도 안 되는군요.
Risk it!	모험해 봐!
Same as you.	너하고 같아.
Same to you.	당신도요.
Save face.	체면 좀 지키세요.
Say your piece.	소신껏 말해.
Seasoning's Greeting!	새해 복 많이 받으세요!
See you at school.	학교에서 보자.
Settle down back there.	거기서 잠잠히 있어라.
Shake a leg.	서둘러.
She blew her top.	그녀는 머리끝까지 화가 났어.
She deserved what she got.	그녀가 자초했어요.
She has a big mouth.	그녀는 입이 싸요.
She has a lot of style.	그녀는 품위가 있다.
She has got someone on the side.	그녀는 따로 만나는 사람이 있어.
She is all legs.	그녀는 키가 커.
She is hot.	그녀는 매력적이야.
She is two-faced.	그녀는 이중인격자야.
She likes to talk big.	그녀는 과장해서 말해.
She looked weird.	그녀가 이상하게 보여.
She sits up and takes notice.	많이 좋아지고 있어.(환자의 건강상태)
She wearing braces.	그녀는 치열 교정기를 하고 있다.
She's a good talker.	말이 청산유수로군.
She's dumped me.	그녀가 나를 찼어.
She's very moody.	그녀는 변덕이 심해.

Show me!	증명해 봐요!
Simmer down.	흥분을 가라앉혀.
Since when?	언제부터?
Snap out of it.	꿈 깨.
So what?	그래서 어쨌다고?
Something's come up.	일이 생겼어요.
Sometimes your criticism is too much.	가끔 네 비판이 지나쳐.
Sorry for causing you so much trouble.	많은 폐를 끼쳐서 죄송해요.
Sounds like they're overcharging you for labor!	수고료가 너무 과한 것 아니냐!
Stand a little to the left.	조금 왼쪽으로 서세요.
Stand by.	대기해.
Start the car.	차에 시동 걸어.
Step aside!	비켜!
Step on it, please.	빨리 가주세요.
Step on it.	속도를 좀 내세요.
Stop before someone gets hurt.	누구 다치기 전에 그만들 하시오.
Stop criticizing me!	나 그만 비판해.
Stop flipping channels.	채널 좀 그만 돌리렴.
Stop passing notes in class.	수업 중에 쪽지 돌리지 마세요.
Stop talking to your partner.	옆 사람과 이야기하지 마세요.
Support me for a while.	나 좀 도와줘봐.
Sure, I'll be there.	꼭 갈게.
Swallow your pride.	자존심은 버려.
Take a free sample.	무료상품을 가져가세요.
Take everything.	맘대로 하세요.

Take it again.	다시 찍어 주세요.
Take your pick.	고르세요.
Talk about biting the hand that feeds you.	배은망덕도 유분수다.
Tell me what happened.	무슨 일이 있었는지 말해봐.
Tell me what you feel.	어떻게 생각하는지 말해봐.
Thank you for the praise.	칭찬해 주시니 감사합니다.
Thanks for the lift.	태워주셔서 감사합니다.
Thanks for your time.	시간 내 주셔서 감사합니다.
That explains a lot.	그거 많은 의미가 있어.
That was my best time.	그때가 가장 행복했어요.
That's a good buy.	싸게 사시는 겁니다.
That's a keen observation.	아주 예리한 관찰력이군요.
That's a lovely thought!	정말 좋은 생각이야.
That's a private matter.	그건 비밀이지.
That's a rip off.	바가지 쓰셨군요.
That's about it.	대충 그랬어.
That's another pair of shoes.	그건 딴 얘기다.
That's awesome!	굉장한데!
That's icing on the cake.	금상첨화다.
That's just an excuse.	그건 변명에 지나지 않아.
That's nice of you, but maybe some other time.	고맙긴 한데 다음에 하자.
That's not the end of the line.	새치기하지 마세요.
That's really super!	엄청나네요.
That's the deal!	그러자.

That's the name of the game.	그것이 핵심이야.
That's the question.	그게 의문점이야.
That's too steep for me.	저에게 너무 비싸요.
The buses run every 20 minutes.	버스는 매 20분마다 운행합니다.
The engine keeps overheating.	엔진이 계속 가열돼요.
The expiration date has passed.	유효기간이 지났어.
The news has really gotten me down.	그 소식을 들으니 정말 우울해진다.
The price is right.	가격이 적당하다.
The sooner we start, the easier it will be.	빨리 시작할수록 일이 쉬어질 거야.
The test is open book.	책을 참조해도 좋아요.
The test will be timed.	시험은 시간제한이 있을 겁니다.
The tires are getting old.	타이이기 낡았어요.
There are no complications.	합병증은 없어요.
There is a fly in the ointment.	옥에 티다.
There is a lot of blood.	피가 많이 나요.
There is a shared kitchen on each floor.	각 층에 공동 주방이 있다.
There might be another way.	다른 방법이 있을 거야.
There must be an accident.	사고가 난 것이 틀림없어.
There's no need to hurry.	서두를 필요가 없어요.
There's no reason for you to be upset.	네가 화낼 이유는 없어.
There's not much time.	시간이 많지 않아.
There's not such things as a free lunch!	세상에 공짜가 없다.
These are a perfect fit.	딱 맞아요.
These are for you.	이거 너한테 주는 거야.

They always hang out together.	그들은 어울려 다녀.
They are for the birds.	시시해.
They aren't matched very well.	서로 안 어울려.
They never have what I want.	내가 원하는 것은 없어.
They sent me a rejection letter.	그들이 입학 거부서를 보냈어요.
They're going to be here any minute.	그들이 당장이라도 올텐데.
Things like that really drive me crazy.	그런 일은 날 미치게 만든다.
Think nothing of it.	별거 아닙니다.
This beer is flat.	이 맥주 김이 빠졌어.
This doesn't involve you.	넌 이 일에 상관없어.
This dress is kinky.	이 옷은 속이 다 비쳐.
This fare's much higher than usual.	평소보다 많이 나왔어요.
This is a little something for you.	조그만 선물입니다.
This is a shocking experience!	이건 충격적인 경험이야!
This is a towaway zone.	이곳은 주차 견인지역입니다.
This is all very sudden for me.	좀 당황스럽네요.
This is light?	이것이 심심풀이라고?
This is not good.	이러면 안 되는데.
This is our moment.	이제 우리의 시간이야.
This is totally insane.	이건 정말 어리석은 거야.
This is what I always wear.	이것이 제가 항상 입는 것입니다.
This just came in.	방금 이게 왔더군.
This problem runs in my family.	가족 내력입니다.
This service here is awful.	이곳 서비스는 형편없어.
This year really went by fast.	한 해 정말 빨리 지나갔다.
Time to pack.	짐 쌀 시간이야.

Time will tell.	시간이 약이야.
Time's up.	시간이 다 됐습니다.
To you and me!	너와의 우정을 위해.
Tomorrow is another day.	내일은 새로운 날이 시작될 거야.
Traffic is murder at this time of day.	하루 중 이 시간에 교통체증이 심해.
Try to be in class on time.	정각에 참여하도록 하세요.
Tuition is going up again.	수업료가 또 인상된대요.
Turn around.	돌아보시오.
Turn in the paper next week.	다음 주에 보고서를 제출해 주세요.
Use your imagination.	머리 좀 써라.
Waste of bloody time.	귀중한 시간을 낭비하는 거야.
Watch your language!	말조심해.
Wax your car after washing it well.	잘 닦으신 후에 광을 내세요.
We are losing precious time!	시간 낭비하지 맙시다!
We are only stopping here for 5 minutes.	여기서 5분 정차합니다.
We don't have that many left.	남아 있는 게 별로 없어요.
We had a real nice time.	정말 즐거웠어요.
We have a lot in common.	우리는 통하는 게 많아.
We have plenty of time.	우리는 시간이 많아요.
We have to cut costs.	비용을 줄여야 합니다.
We have to get together more often.	이제 좀 더 자주 만나자.
We must be getting close.	가까워지고 있나봐.
We must go ahead.	우리는 계속해야 돼.
We need gas.	기름 좀 넣어야겠어요.
We need to have a little chat.	우리 잠깐 얘기 좀 하자.

We'd better see what's up.	어떻게 되는지 두고 보자.
We're short of time.	시간이 없어요.
We've missed it.	놓쳐 버렸어.
What a change!	대단한 변화예요.
What a coincidence!	와 세상 좁구나.
What and incredible feeling!	도무지 믿어지지 않아!
What are friends for?	친구 좋다는 게 뭐야.
What are the most famous tourist attractions?	가장 유명한 관광명소들은 어디죠?
What are the show times?	공연시간은 언제죠?
What are these buttons for?	이 버튼은 무슨 용도죠?
What are you doing tonight?	오늘 저녁에 뭐할 건가요?
What are your hours?	영업시간이 언제입니까?
What classes did you sign up for this term?	이번 학기에 어떤 수업을 신청했어요?
What did she look like?	그 여자는 어떻게 생겼는데요?
What do you do when you're free?	시간 날 때 뭐하죠?
What do you feel like eating?	뭐 먹고 싶니?
What do you mean by that?	무슨 말이죠?
What do you want from me?	나한테 원하는 게 뭐죠?
What does it have to do with you?	그게 너와 무슨 상관이지?
What does that abbreviation stand for?	그 약자가 무엇을 나타내지요?
What for?	무엇 때문에?
What have you been doing?	그동안 어떻게 지내셨어요?
What hours are the library open?	도서관 열람시간이 몇 시죠?

What is the highest level of education that you have received?	최종학력이 뭐죠?
What is this regarding?	무슨 일이죠?
What is your paper on?	보고서는 무엇에 관한 것인가요?
What kind of game is this?	이게 무슨 장난이죠?
What made you so afraid?	뭐가 널 그렇게 무서워하게 만들었니?
What number are you calling?	몇 번으로 전화하셨니요?
What position do you hold?	직책은?
What seems to be the problem?	무슨 일 있나요?
What seems to be the trouble?	어디가 문제죠?
What time do you call it a day?	몇 시에 퇴근해요?
What times are the classes?	수업이 몇 시에 있나요?
What was I saying?	무슨 얘기 했지?
What was the fuss all about?	무엇 때문에 그렇게 소란이야?
What was your response?	당신 반응은?
What will my future be?	내 미래는 어떻게 될까?
What's going on?	어떻게 된거죠?
What's on the test?	시험에 뭐가 나오죠?
What's on your mind?	뭐 신경 쓰는 거라도 있니?
What's the admission fee?	입장료는 얼마죠?
What's the big idea?	도대체 무슨 생각이니?
What's the fastest meal I can eat?	가장 빨리되는 음식이 뭐죠?
What's the rate for a compact?	소형차는 얼마죠?(렌트)
What've you done?	당신 무슨 짓을 한 거야?
Whatever you say.	얼마든지요.
When are you?	언제가 예정일이니?

When can I get the test result?	언제 검사결과를 알죠?
When can we get a table?	언제 자리가 나죠?
When can we meet?	언제 만나면 되나요?
When is it good through?	언제까지 유효하나요?
When is the housewarming party?	집들이는 언제 하죠?
When is the test?	시험이 언제죠?
When was this picture taken?	이 사진은 언제 찍었니?
When will you get there?	언제 도착하나요?
When you're finished with the test please bring it to the front.	시험을 끝내면 앞으로 제출해 주세요.
Where are the others?	나머지는 어디 있지?
Where are you going from here?	이제 무엇을 할 예정이죠?
Where can I pay for these things?	어디서 계산하죠?
Where could I find a book on English linguistics?	영어 언어학에 관한 책은 어디에서 찾을 수 있죠?
Where could I have put it?	내가 도대체 그걸 어디다 둔 거지?
Where does this street lead?	이 길은 어디가 나오죠?
Where was I?	어디까지 얘기했지?
Where's the fitting room?	어디서 갈아입죠?
Where's the latch for the gas tank cover?	주유구 개폐장치는 어디 있나요?
Whether you make it or not.	당신이 그것을 만들든 말든.
Who cares about it?	까짓거 뭐.
Who cares?	알게 뭐야?
Who comes to mind?	누가 떠오르지?
Who do you think you are?	당신 분수나 아세요?

Who has a question about the assignment?	숙제에 관해 질문 있나요?
Who is this?	어디시죠?(전화상)
Who is to blame?	누구 잘못이지?
Who wants to go first?	누가 먼저 하고 싶어요?
Who's in charge?	책임자가 누구죠?
Who's plotting them?	누가 그런 것을 꾸며요?
Whose side are you on?	너 누구 편이냐?
Why are you always like that?	넌 왜 맨날 그 모양이니?
Why are you talking about me behind my back?	왜 험담하고 다니니?
Why didn't you go after him?	왜 안 따라갔어?
Why do you look so miserable?	왜 그렇게 슬픈 표정이니?
Why don't you ask somebody for directions?	누군가에게 길을 물어보는 게 어때?
Why don't you guys cool down?	둘 다 진정 좀 하는 게 어때?
Why the long face?	왜 실망스러운 얼굴이니?
Will I need an operation?	수술이 필요합니까?
Will you please go now, and leave me alone?	제발 날 좀 내버려둬요.
With whose permission?	누구 마음대로?
Would you like a taste?	맛 좀 볼래?
Would you like me to carry that for you?	제가 짐을 날라드릴까요?
Would you mind backing up, please?	뒤로 좀 빼주실래요?
Would you mind giving me a tour?	구경시켜 주실래요?
Would you mind taking our picture?	사진 좀 찍어 주실래요?

Would you please hear me out?	내 말 좀 들어봐요.
Yes and no.	한마디로 안 돼. (판단이나 설명이 어려울 때)
You always say that.	언제나 그런 식으로 말하지.
You are a cut above me.	네가 한수 위야.
You are on the fast track.	잘나가는 구나.
You better take this.	넌 이걸 잡고 있는 게 좋을 거다.
You can count on me.	저를 믿으세요.
You can pay next time.	다음에 네가 사.
You can reach me at my office.	사무실로 연락주세요.
You can't be touched.	접근 못할 거야.
You can't judge a book by its cover.	외모로 판단하지 마.
You can't miss it.	찾기 쉬울 겁니다.
You didn't send enough.	충분히 보내지 않았어요.
You don't have to answer right away.	바로 대답할 필요 없어.
You don't have to be precise.	정확히 말할 필요 없어요.
You dropped the ball.	네가 잘못한 거지.
You feel like you're alone.	너는 혼자라는 것을 느끼고 있군.
You flatter!	과찬이야!
You got dirt on your nose by the way.	넌 코에 뭐가 묻었다.
You got it backwards.	넌 그 반대로 알았어.
You have a fifty-fifty chance.	승산은 반이다.
You have to refresh my memory.	기억이 잘 안나요.
You haven't changed a bit!	여전하네.
You hit the nail on the head.	정곡을 찔렀어.
You like it?	그거 마음에 드니?

You lined your pockets.	네가 횡령했어.
You make a good couple.	둘 다 좋은 연인입니다.
You messed up.	네가 일을 망쳤어.
You might be seeing this on a future test.	다음 시험에 나올지도 몰라요.
You missed a charge here.	청구금액이 빠진 게 있네요.
You missed the boat.	한 발 늦었어.
You must have taken a shortcut.	당신은 지름길을 택했군.
You name it.	말만 하세요.
You need a ride?	태워드릴까요?
You need authorization.	허가기 필요합니다.
You owe me.	너 빚졌어.
You possess many of qualities.	넌 많은 소질들을 가지고 있어.
You read my mind.	내 마음을 잘 아네.
You really came through.	네가 해냈구나.
You really caused me a lot of sorrow.	당신은 정말 내게 너무 많은 슬픔을 줬어요.
You really frustrated me.	너 정말 날 답답하게 하는구나.
You really get under my skin.	성깔 건드리는군.
You say something.	뭐라고 말 좀 해보세요.
You should know your place.	분수를 아세요.
You should've been there to see it.	너도 그것을 봤어야 했어.
You smell of the shop.	장사꾼 냄새가 나.
You stood me up.	날 바람맞혔어.
You will pay for this.	후회할거야.
You'll feel better soon.	곧 나아질 겁니다.
You'll get through this.	너는 이겨낼 거야.

You're a life saver.	당신은 생명의 은인이야.
You're almost there.	거의 다 왔습니다.
You're going to pay for what you said.	네가 한 말에 대가를 치룰 거야.
You're good friends.	두 분이 친한가 봐요?
You're holding everyone up.	너 때문에 못하고 있어.
You're in no condition to drive.	당신은 운전할 상태가 아니야.
You're nobody.	너는 별볼일 없어.
You're not my friend anymore.	넌 더 이상 내 친구가 아니야.
You're not oppressed.	너 우울증은 아니지.
You're pushing it.	너 너무 몰아붙인다.
You're sneaking it.	뭔가 감추고 있지.
You're so shortsighted.	당신 근시안적인 사람이군.
You're soaked.	흠뻑 젖었군요.
You're the best of the group.	네가 이 그룹에서 최고야.
You've come a long way.	대단한 발전을 하셨군요.
You've dug your own grave.	넌 스스로 무덤을 팠어.
You've got somebody behind you.	너 믿는 구석이 있구나.
You've got that backwards.	정반대로 알고 있구나.
You've made a mistake.	뭔가 실수하고 계시는 거예요?
You've mentioned it.	들었어요.
You've taken a great load off my mind!	큰 걱정을 덜었답니다.
Your guess is as good as mine.	나도 모르지.
Your wish is my command.	말씀하시는 대로 다 해드리겠습니다.
Yourself?	너는?

IV

Fast Reading skill

IV Fast Reading skill

skill 1 문장의 기본골격 파악

영어 문장은 핵심 구성요소와 그에 따른 부가적 요소로 구성되어 있다. 먼저 핵심 구성요소는 문장을 형성시키기 위해서 빼서는 안 되는 주어와 동사이고 좀 더 확장이 되면 보어와 목적어가 있고 부가적 요소로 수식어, 접속어, 독립어가 있다.

1. 다음 문장에서 기본골격을 표시해 보자.

＊ The little girl / is very patient.
주어 부분 / 술어 부분

＊ The children / are running / around on a new rug.
주어 부분 / 술어 부분 / 부가어

2. 구체적으로 주어, 동사, 목적어, 보어 등을 표시해 보자.

＊ I / contributed / many books / to the library.
주어 / 동사 / 목적어 / 부가어

＊ Surfing / is / quite / the thing / there.
주어 / 동사 / 부사 / 보어 / 부사

3. 문장의 기본 구성은 다음과 같다.

* 주어 + 동사
* 주어 + 동사 + 보어
* 주어 + 동사 + 목적어
* 주어 + 동사 + 간접목적어 + 직접목적어
* 주어 + 동사 + 목적어 + 목적격보어 外

4. 문장에서 부사, 부사구, 부사절이 쓰이는 이유는 문장의 의미 확대와 상황설정 때문이다.

* The waiter smiled <u>politely</u> <u>as he handed me my bill.</u>

부사 부사절

5. 도식

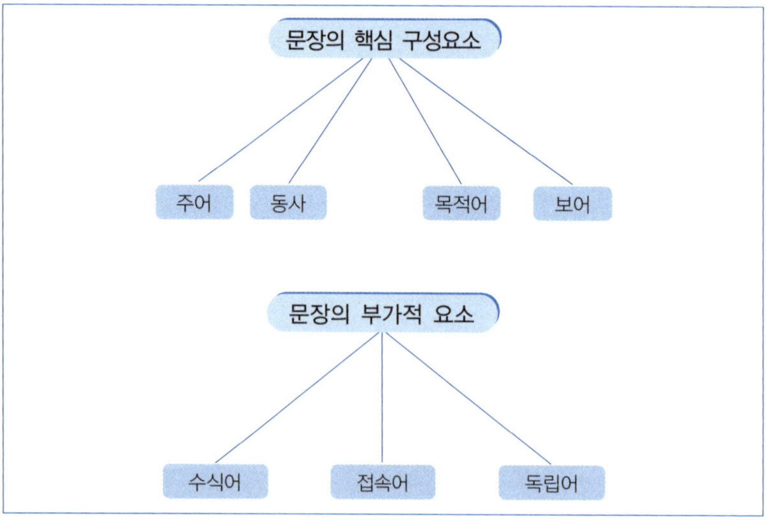

Test 1

다음 각 문장을 기본골격으로 나누고 해석하시오.

1. The job must be done in a hurry.

2. Please don't horn in our conversation. * horn in 끼워 들다

3. The majority of factories in the region have a workforce of 50 to 100.

4. The pieces on display are often borrowed from another museum or private collection.

5. You can't lock your suitcase because there is a bit of clothes sticking out.

6. The little girl is riding backwards.

7. Load this box with all the clothing you can get into it.

___

8. You can park your stroller here.

___

9. It is a bitter cold and windy today.

___

해석

1. 그 일은 서둘러서 마무리 돼야 한다.
2. 대화에 끼어들지 마세요.
3. 그 지역의 대부분의 공장은 50에서 100 정도의 인부가 있다.
4. 전시중에 있는 작품은 종종 다른 박물관이나 개인에게서 빌려 온 것이다.
5. 천이 좀 나와 있어서 여행가방을 잠글 수 없어요.
6. 그 소녀는 거꾸로 타고 있다.
7. 가능한 한 모든 옷을 이 상자에 넣어라.
8. 여기에다 유모차를 놓으셔도 돼요.
9. 오늘은 매우 춥고 바람이 심해.

Test 2

다음 지문에서 문장의 골격을 파악하시오.

It is very important for a small child to learn how to take charge of his or her health.

Proper nutrition, fresh air, regular chances to run around, and lots of love and attention all contribute to a child's mental, physical, and emotional well-being. Going to the dentist, the doctor or a well-baby clinic at least once a year is also an important part of a kid's maintenance program.

해석 어린이도 자신의 건강을 돌보는 법을 배워야 한다. 적당한 영양 섭취, 신선한 공기, 규칙적으로 뛰어노는 것, 넘치는 사랑과 애정, 이 모든 것이 어린아이의 정신적, 신체적, 감정적 안정에 기여한다. 또한 최소 일 년에 한 번은 아이들을 데리고 치과나 의사, 소아 진료소에 찾아가는 것은 아이들의 건강유지를 위해 중요하다.

skill 2 의미단위 파악(끊어 읽기)

우리가 말을 할 때 연속적으로 쉬지 않고 말을 하는 사람은 없다. 이것은 의미를 명확히 전달하기 위함이다. 마찬가지로 독해를 할 때에도 문장의 주요소와 부가적 요소를 잘 파악한 다음 끊어 읽기를 해야 한다.

1. 주부가 긴 문장은 주어와 동사를 파악한다.

* The fact that she is attractive/ is true.

* His out-of-pocket expenses for his trip/ were for the bus fare and for food.

2. 구와 절의 앞, 뒤에서 끊는다.

* Tell you what,/ buy three of them,/ and I'll knock ten dollars /off the total.

3. 부사절, 부사구가 오면 뒤에서 끊고 주어를 찾으면 된다.

* In a test market this fall,/ they're going to release the product.

4. 도식

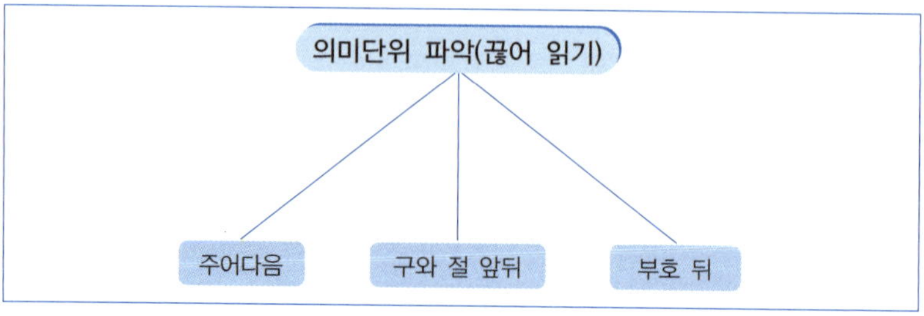

Test 1

다음 각 문장을 의미단위로 끊고 해석하시오.

1. She's taking a year off and then going back.

____

2. We are expecting a lot of applicants for the job.

____

3. She set up chairs and tables for the party.

____

4. The stolen goods were stashed away in a warehouse.

____

5. The lack of computing facilities in the office frustrated him.

____

6. The date for the meeting is now definite.

____

7. The noise turned out to be just the cat scratching at the door.

____

8. Do you think she will make it as a doctor?

____

9. The students complained that they were being penalized by the new rules.

____

해석

1. 한 해 휴학한 후 복학할 것이다.
2. 그 일에 많은 사람들이 지원할거야.
3. 그녀가 파티를 위해 테이블과 의자를 준비하고 있다.
4. 그 훔친 물건은 창고에 치워졌다. *stash=hide
5. 사무실의 계산시스템은 그를 좌절시켰다.
6. 회의 날짜는 명확하다.
7. 그 소음은 단지 고양이가 문을 긁는 소리임이 드러났다.
8. 그녀가 의사로서 해낼 것이라 생각하나요?
9. 그 학생들은 자신들이 새로운 규칙에 의해 벌을 받는 것에 불평했다.

Test 2

다음 지문을 의미 단위(끊어 읽기)로 나타내시오.

Buying the right gift for people you know well requires time and effort compared to buying for a casual acquaintance where you can set a cash limit.

Close friends and family appreciate it so much when the gift is something they would have picked out for themselves or had wanted and couldn't afford. Usually, gift selection is not a simple matter of walking into a department store and exiting within 2 or3 minutes with purchase in hand. For another thing, people close to you have an unspoken expectation that you know what they want, so you have to be a mind reader. Would they like clothing, a book, or hobby stuff?

해석 그저 가벼운 친분이 있는 사람들에게 정해 놓은 액수에 맞춰 선물을 사는 것에 비해 잘 아는 사람들에게 줄 적절한 선물을 고르는 것은 시간과 노력을 요하는 일입니다. 가까운 친구들이나 가족들은 자신들이 직접 골랐을 것 같은 것이나, 사고 싶었지만 살 여유가 없었던 선물을 받았을 때 매우 고마워합니다. 대개 선물을 고르는 일은 백화점에 들어가서 2, 3분 있다가 물건을 집어 들고 나오는 단순한 문제가 아닙니다. 또 하나의 문제는 친한 사람들은 당신이 자신들이 원하는 것을 알고 있으리라는 무언의 기대를 갖고 있기 때문에 당신은 독심술가가 되어야 한다는 점입니다. 그 사람들이 옷, 책 또는 취미용품을 맘에 들어 할까요?

skill 3 필요한 부분만 읽기

영어시험에서 독해 지문을 접근하는 방식은 2가지이다. 첫째, 지문을 내려읽고 문제를 보는 경우 둘째, 문제를 먼저 보고 해당부분만 읽는 경우이다. 선택지에서 답을 고를 때 지문과 동떨어지거나 부분적인 의미만 맞는 것은 물론 정답이 될 수 없다.

1. 지문을 읽으면서 대강의 내용을 파악한다.

2. 구체적인 사항은 일일이 기억하려 하지 말자.

3. 글의 구성이 어떠한 구조로 되어있는지 파악한다.

4. 연결어에 의해 의미변화가 이루어지는지 파악한다.
   * but, however, yet은 특히 중요하다.

5. scanning을 하면서 처음 두, 세 문장에 중점을 둔다.
   * 일반적으로 영어문장은 여기에 주제가 들어 있다.

6. 일반적으로 영어는 3단 구성이 원칙이다.
   * 주제문(subject sentence)
   * 서술문(supporting sentence)–다양한 전개방식이 등장한다.
   * 결론문(concluding sentence)

7. 문단은 통일성, 일관성, 연결성의 특성을 가지고 있다.
   * 각 문장은 별개의 것이 아니라 하나의 주제를 향한 논리적 연결체이다.

Test 1

다음 지문을 scanning하고 대강의 줄거리를 쓰시오.

The college years are not only a time for academics, but a time of self-discovery. Colleges offer many activities outside of the lecture hall. There are social events, as simple as unorganized fun in a dormitory to concerts given by famous musicians. There are chances to get involved in national and international politics, from working for a political party to staging a demonstration against forced labor.

줄거리

해석 대학 시절은 학문을 위한 시간일 뿐 아니라 자기 발견의 시간이기도 하다. 대학에는 강의실 밖에서 이루어지는 활동들이 많다. 여기에는 기숙사에서 즉흥적으로 벌어지는 재미거리처럼 간단한 것에서부터 유명한 음악인들이 벌이는 콘서트 등의 다양한 사회행사가 있다. 국가적, 국제적인 정치행사에 참여할 기회도 있는데, 어떤 정당의 편에서 일한다거나 강제노동에 반발하는 시위운동을 선동하는 것이 이에 해당된다.

Test 2

다음 지문을 읽고 T, F값을 정하시오.

Choking is sometimes caused by swallowing a large piece of food or a small toy. If the airway is only partly blocked, the person may still be able to cough. If the cough is strong, the person may be able to cough up what he has swallowed. If he cannot, however, you must help.

1. Choking is caused by swallowing a large toy.

____

2. If the airway is only partly blocked, the person may not be able to cough.

____

해석 질식은 때로 커다란 음식 덩어리나 작은 장난감을 삼켰을 때 일어난다. 만약 기도가 완전히 막히지 않았다면, 그 사람은 여전히 기침을 할 수 있을 것이다. 그 기침이 세면 그 사람은 삼킨 것을 토해 낼 수 있다. 그러나 삼킨 것을 토해 낼 수 없다면 당신이 도와야 한다.

1. 질식은 커다란 장난감을 삼켜서 일어난다.
2. 만약 기도가 부분적으로 막혔을 때, 그 사람은 기침할 가능성이 없을 수도 있다.

skill 4 추론

일반적으로 독해는 두 가지로 구성된다. 첫째는 읽으면서 의미가 순순히 전달되는 사실적 독해, 둘째는 주어진 지문을 바탕으로 논리적, 추론적 사고를 요하는 추론적 독해이다. 추론에 대한 리딩스킬을 알아보도록 하자.

1. 반드시 지문에 근거한 추론을 한다.

2. 전체적인 문맥 속에서 파악하려 한다.

3. 익숙한 지문 내용이라고 해서 자신의 배경지식만 믿고 대해서는 안 된다.

4. 지문을 읽으면서 다음에 나올 내용을 생각해본다.

5. 첫 문장에 빈칸이 보이거나, 결론을 나타내는 연결사(in brief, in short, therefore, so)가 이끄는 마지막 문장에 빈칸이 있는 것은 **요지를 추론**하는 유형의 문제이다.

6. **주제문**을 통한 세부사항 추론을 알아보자.

주제문 : You should protect the air.

세부사항 :

＊ One, by combining your daily errands into one sensible trip.

※ Two, by maintaining your car and keeping it in top running condition to save money and eliminate traffic congestion.

주제문을 통해 관련된 세부사항이 나오면 답으로 정한다.

7. 전후관계를 통한 세부사항 추론이 있다.

※ The star received several ______ messages from unnamed source after she accepted the offer to direct the controversial film.

빈칸에 알맞은 것을 고르시오.

① threatening ② happy ③ through ④ normal

8. 도식

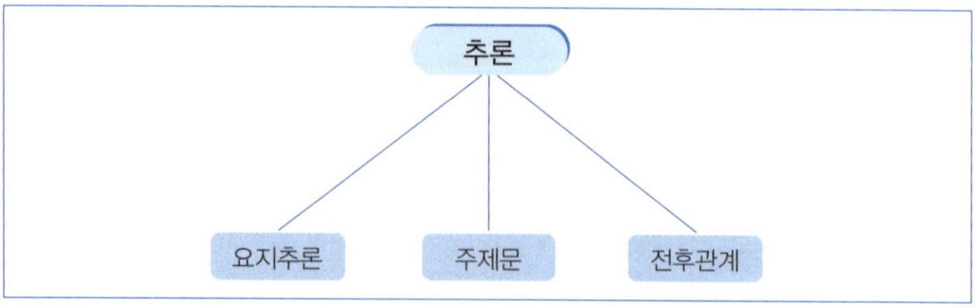

Test 1

빈칸에 들어갈 단어를 고르시오.

Highway robbery has always existed in the world, but it seems that either it is getting worse than ever or people are simply travelling more than they ever have and are statistically more vulnerable to it. It is also getting more common to hear about stolen items from hotel rooms by hotel employees who think they have more to gain from a large theft than permanent employment at low ______.

① wages ② charge ③ fare ④ height

해석 노상강도는 늘 있어 왔다. 하지만 전보다 더 심해진 것 같은데, 이는 단순히 사람들이 예전보다 여행을 더 많이 해서 통계적으로 그렇게 나타나는 것일 수도 있다. 또한 호텔 직원이 객실에서 물건을 훔친다는 이야기도 왕왕 들려온다. 이들은 적은 월급을 받으면서 평생 이런 직장에 있는 것보다 한 판 크게 터지는 것이 얻을 게 더 많다고 생각한다.

skill 5 주제문 찾기

어떤 글을 쓸 때는 목적이 있다. 목적은 주제를 통해 나타나기 마련이다. 주제문은 전체 글을 요약하고 논지가 명확히 드러나는 문장이다.

1. 주제문은 처음 한 두 문장이나 마지막 문장에 드러난다.

2. 결론을 나타내는 연결사 뒤에 위치할 가능성이 있다.
   * thus, so, therefore, hence, in short, in brief, in conclusion

3. 너무 포괄적인 문장은 주제문이 될 수 없다.

4. 글의 일반구성이 주제문-서술문-결론문이거나, 도입부-서술문-주제문의 특성을 띤다.

5. 역접의 연결사 다음의 문장에 비중을 둔다.
   * however, in contrast, on the other hand, but, on the contrary

6. 지문에서 반복적으로 사용하는 단어가 무엇인지 파악한다.

7. 주제문 형태 : 주제문이 명시된 경우와 전체에 함축된 경우가 있다.
   글 : 명시 글, 함축 글

Test 1

다음 지문을 해석하고 주제를 쓰시오.

It would be costly not to use your language properly. Your language influences others, and their reactions to you may be determined by it. For example, your language use affects your teachers' attitudes toward you. It affects your parents' responses to your requests. It can also affect your friends' understanding of you and their feelings toward you. It may even determine your ability to get a particular job or move to a higher position in your workplace.

Q : What is the main idea? ______________________

해석 언어를 올바르게 사용하지 않는다면 그 대가를 치르게 될 것이다. 당신의 언어는 타인에게 영향을 미치고, 당신에 대한 그들의 반응은 그 언어에 의해 결정된다. 예를 들어, 당신의 언어 사용은 당신에 대한 선생님의 태도에 영향을 미칠 것이다. 그것은 당신의 요구에 대한 부모님의 반응에 영향을 미친다. 또한 당신 친구들의 당신에 대한 이해와 당신에 대한 그들의 감정에도 영향을 미칠 수 있다. 언어는 심지어 특정한 일자리를 얻거나 직장에서 승진하는 당신의 능력까지도 결정할 수 있다.

Test 2

다음 지문을 해석하고 주제를 쓰시오.

Most children are excellent language learners. They can learn a second language quickly and easily. Most adults, on the other hand, find learning a second language difficult. They must study hard, and it usually takes them a long time to master the language. Adults usually try to learn a second language the same way they lean mathematics, science, history, or other subjects; but children learn a second language the same way they learned their first language. The child language learners has all the necessary skills to learn another language, but the adult language learner often has to relearn these skills in order to learn a second language.

Q : What is the primary purpose of the passage?

____

해석 어린이는 대부분 뛰어난 언어학습자들이다. 어린이들은 제2언어를 신속하고 쉽게 배울 수 있다. 반면에, 대부분의 어른들은 제2언어를 배우는 것이 어렵다는 것을 알게 된다. 어른들은 열심히 공부해야 되고, 언어를 마스터하는 데는 항상 오랜 시간이 걸린다. 어른들은 늘 제2언어를 수학이나 과학, 역사 등 다른 과목들은 공부하는 방식으로 학습하려고 애쓴다. 그러나 어린아이들은 모국어를 배운 방식으로 제2언어를 배운다. 어린이 언어학습자는 또 다른 언어를 배우는 데 필요한 모든 기술을 가지고 있지만, 성인 언어학습자는 제2언어를 배우기 위해 이 기술을 다시 배워야 한다.

skill 6 비판적 읽기

지문을 읽어 나갈 때 아무런 생각 없이 읽기만 해서는 도저히 그 내용을 100% 이해할 수는 없다. 따라서 작자의 논지를 파악하려고 하면서 자신의 비판적 사고가 들어가야 한다.

1. 자신이 지문의 주인공이 되어보자.

2. 단순한 읽을거리로 대하지 말고 요약과 체계화를 통해 자신의 것으로 만들어 보자.

3. 읽은 내용을 기억하려고 노력하자.

4. 수험 때가 아니면 읽은 내용을 2, 3번 반복해서 읽어도 좋다.

5. 평소 영어학습이라면 나름대로 지문의 옆 공란에 자신의 생각을 기술해도 좋다.

6. 글쓴이의 논지 전개와 내용의 연관관계를 따져보자.

7. 평소 영자신문의 사설을 통해 사고력과 논리력을 키워보자.

8. 행간을 읽어라.

9. 사실적 이해를 묻는 지문인지 추론적 이해를 묻는 문제인지 파악해 본다.

Test 1

다음 지문을 해석하고 자신의 비판적 사고 내용을 쓰시오.

One of the benefits in my brother's company is a day off for employees' birthdays. Although it seemed unlikely that my company would start the same plan., I decided to ask. My boss listened to my words carefully. And then he said, If anyone deserves the day off on your birthday, it's your mother.

비판적 사고

해석 나의 동생이 다니는 회사의 혜택 중 하나는 사원들의 생일 날 하루 쉬게 해 주는 것이다. 내가 다니는 회사도 똑같은 계획을 시작할 것 같지는 않았지만, 나는 요청하기로 결심했다. 사장은 내 말을 주의 깊게 들었다. 그런 다음 그는 "당신 생일날 하루 쉴 자격이 있는 사람이 있다면 그 사람은 당신의 어머니요."라고 말했다.

Test 2

다음 지문을 해석하고 문장의 중의성을 파악해 보시오.

Claire always wanted to be a singer. But, to tell the truth, she had a terrible voice. She took lessons and practiced every day. In spite of all this, her voice didn't improve. Her teacher finally gave up and stopped the lessons, but Claire refused to quit and kept practicing. One day she decided to give a concert and invited her former teacher to attend. The teacher was very worried about what to say about the concert. She knew it would be awful and it was. She didn't want to tell a lie, but she didn't hurt Claire's feelings either. Finally she got an idea and went backstage to greet Claire. "How was my concert tonight?" Claire asked. "My dear," said the teacher, "<u>you'll never be better than you were tonight.</u>" "Really, That is really kind of you to say so." Claire said.

Q : What does the underlined sentence imply?

____

해석 클레어는 항상 가수가 되고 싶어했다. 하지만 사실대로 말하자면 그녀의 목소리는 끔찍했다. 그녀는 매일 교습을 받고 연습을 했다. 그러나 이 모든 것에도 불구하고 그녀의 목소리는 좋아지지 않았다. 그녀의 선생님도 마침내 포기하고 교습을 그만두었다. 하지만 클레어는 그만두지 않고 연습을 계속했다. 어느 날 그녀는

계속 ☞

해석 음악회를 열기로 결심하고는 옛 선생님께 참석해 달라고 청했다. 선생님은 그 음악회에 대해 뭐라고 말을 해야 할지 걱정이 되었다. 그녀는 음악회가 끔찍할 것임을 알고 있었고, 실제로 그러했다. 그녀는 거짓말을 하기도 싫었고, 클레어의 기분을 상하게 하고 싶지도 않았다. 마침내 그녀는 좋은 생각이 떠올랐고 클레어에게 인사하기 위해 무대 뒤편으로 갔다. 클레어는 "오늘밤 제 음악회가 어땠나요?"라고 물었다. 선생님은 "애야, 너는 오늘밤보다 더 잘할 수는 없을 거다."라고 말했다. "정말요? 그렇게 말씀해 주셔서 정말 감사합니다."라고 클레어는 말했다.

skill 7 배경지식 활용하기

평소에 독서습관을 키워 놓는 것이 독해에 커다란 도움이 된다. 물론 그렇다고 무턱대고 많은 양의 글을 읽으라는 얘기는 아니다. 양질의 글을 선택해서 사고력과 배경지식을 쌓아야 한다.

1. 신문은 꼭 읽자.

2. 독해 지문은 다양한 곳에서 출제되기 마련이다. 평소 모든 분야에 관심을 갖자.

3. 배경지식은 주제와 일치하지 않는 경우가 있으니 주어진 지문에 충실해야 한다.

4. 평소 글을 읽으면서 비판과 읽은 기사에 대한 필요한 정보의 기억은 필요하다.

5. 어떤 시험을 준비하느냐에 따라 수험준비가 달라진다. 즉 그에 대한 배경지식도 기출문제를 통해 쌓아야 한다.

Test 1

다음 지문을 해석하고 배경지식을 활용 여부를 체크하시오.

Will cyber schools replace traditional schools some day? In spite of their problems, traditional classrooms hold many advantages over online classes. First of all, traditional classrooms are a place where students may relate one another face to face. That is, a keyboard will never be able to replace the warmth of a handshake, or a monitor the smile of another student. In traditional schools, students may also take part in teamsports, club activities and school festivals-choices net available to students who learn through computers.

배경지식 활용 여부 　　1. Yes 　　2. No

Q : What is the main topic expressed in the passage?

____

해석 가상학교(cyber school)가 언젠가는 전통적인 학교들을 대신할까? 그것들의 문제점에도 불구하고 전통적인 교실들은 온라인 교실들을 능가하는 많은 이점들을 지니고 있다. 무엇보다 먼저 전통적인 교실들은 학생들이 서로 얼굴을 맞대고 이야기 할 수 있는 장소이다. 즉 키보드는 악수의 따뜻함을 대신할 수 없을 것이며, 모니터가 다른 학생들의 미소를 대신할 수 없을 것이다. 전통적인 학교에서 학생들은 컴퓨터를 통해서 배우는 학생들에게 이용되어 질 수 있는 선택적인 팀 스포츠, 클럽활동 그리고 학교 축제에 참여할 수도 있다.

skill 8 재진술 파악

재진술이란 지문 속에 있는 단어나 구, 문장을 다른 표현으로 대치시켜 놓은 것을 말한다. 이렇게 하는 이유는 지문에 대한 정확한 이해를 파악하기 위한 것과 같은 내용을 다르게 표현할 수 있는 능력을 파악하기 위함이다.

1. 지문에 언급된 내용파악을 반영한 예문을 찾는다.
2. 지엽적인 예문은 답이 될 수 없다.
3. 가끔 함정을 두어 약간 변경시켜 놓은 예문도 답이 될 수 없다.
4. 평소 서술방식 변형에 눈여겨본다.
5. 영영사전을 이용하면서 동의어를 파악한다.
6. 다의어에 주의한다.
7. 필수 구문 학습을 평소에 한다.
8. 단어에 대한 사전적 의미와 실제 문장에서의 쓰임에 익숙해지도록 한다.
9. 부분적인 일치보다는 전체문장의 의도와 일치하는 예문을 답으로 한다.

Test 1

다음 지문을 해석하고 올바르게 재진술한 예문을 고르시오.

Examples make abstract ideas more concrete. By putting the right examples in a paragraph or composition, a writer effectively tells his or her idea to a reader.

1. One pictures is worth 1,000 words.
2. The foot of the candle is dark.
3. The end justifies the means.
4. So many man, so many minds.

해석 실례는 추상적인 개념을 보다 구체적으로 만든다. 글에서 적절한 실례를 들어 줌으로써, 작가는 자기의 생각을 효과적으로 독자에게 전달한다.

1. 그림 하나가 천 마디의 말과 같다.
2. 등잔 밑이 어둡다.
3. 목적이 수단을 정당화한다.
4. 각인각색(各人各色)

Test 2

다음 지문을 해석하고 올바르게 재진술한 문장을 고르시오.

Growing as a person may take you to new places and present new challenge. We need efforts to change our lives.

1. 주어진 여건에 만족하라.
2. 도전은 필요하지 않다.
3. 부단한 변화를 시도하라.
4. 감정을 조절하라.

해석 인간으로서 성장한다는 것은 당신을 새로운 장소로 데려가거나 당신에게 새로운 도전을 제시하는 것일 수도 있다.
우리는 삶을 변화시키려는 노력이 필요하다.

Test 3

다음 지문을 해석하고 재진술이 올바른 예문을 찾으시오.

According to ancient lore, every man is born into the world with two bags suspended from his neck-one in front and one behind, and both are full of faults. But the one in front is full of his neighbor's faults; the one behind, full of his own. Consequently, men are blind to their own faults but never lose sight of their neighbor's.

1. There is no place like home
2. The grass is greener on the side of the fence.
3. No work, no money.
4. The pot calls the kettle black.

해석 고대 전설에 의하면, 모든 사람은 목에 두 개의 주머니를 매단 채로-하나는 앞에, 하나는 뒤에-세상에 태어나고, 둘 다 결점들로 가득 차 있다고 한다. 하지만 앞에 있는 주머니는 이웃들의 결점들로 채워져 있고, 뒤에 있는 주머니는 자기 자신의 결점들로 채워져 있다. 결과적으로, 사람들은 자신의 결점은 보지 못하지만, 이웃들의 결점은 결코 놓치지 않는다.

1. 집처럼 편안한 곳은 없다.
2. 남의 떡이 더 커 보인다.
3. 일을 해야 돈을 번다.
4. 냄비가 솥보고 검다고 한다.

skill 9 6하 원칙

주제가 정해지면 글쓴이는 재료를 수집하게 되고 구상과 표현의 과정을 거쳐 글을 완성하게 된다. 이러한 글을 읽을 때에는 6하 원칙에 근거한 파악을 해야 한다.

1. **누가** 등장하는지를 파악하자.
   (주인공 파악)

2. 어떠한 **행위**를 하는지 파악하자.
   (주인공이 구체적으로 하는 행위를 파악)

3. 어떠한 **방법**으로 하는지 파악하자.
   (주인공이 어떤 방법을 이용하는지 파악)

4. **언제**인지 파악하자.
   (관련된 시간이 언제인지 파악)

5. **어디**서 일어났는지 파악하자.
   (장소는 어디인지 파악)

6. **왜** 그러한 것을 하는지 파악하자.
   (사건의 이유가 무엇인지 파악)

Test 1

다음 지문을 읽고 해석하시오. 특히 진하게 된 부분에 집중하여 전체적인 의미를 파악해보시오.

Dictionaries haven't always been on hand to show us the meanings of words we don't know. The first English book that was called a dictionary wasn't written until 1552. And the first English dictionary listing ordinary words as well as difficult words was published in 1702. About 50 years later, the renowned English writer **Samuel Johnson brought out his own dictionary, which he wrote entirely by himself over an eight-year-period! Noah Webster published his first American dictionary in 1806**, with about 40,000 words. In 1828, he brought out another with almost with almost twice as many words. Webster's name still appears on many American dictionaries.

해석 우리가 모르는 단어들의 의미를 알려 주기 위해 사전이 항상 우리 가까이에 있었던 것은 아니었다. 사전이라 불렸던 최초의 영어책은 1552년이 되어서야 출간되었다. 그리고 어려운 어휘뿐만 아니라 보통 수준의 어휘들도 수록했던 최초의 영어사전은 1702년에 출간되었다. 그로부터 약 50년이 지난 후, 저명한 영국의 작가였던 Samuel Johnson이 자신의 사전을 내놓았는데, 그것은 8년이 넘는 기간 동안 전적으로 그 혼자서 썼던 것이었다. Noah Webster는 약 4만 단어가 수록된 첫 미국사전을 1806년에 출간했다. 1828년에 그는 거의 두 배 정도의 어휘가 수록된 또 다른 사전을 펴냈다. Webster의 이름은 아직도 많은 미국사전에서 찾아볼 수 있다.

skill 10 구문식 접근

구문은 지문 파악에 매우 중요한 역할을 한다. 이제까지의 skill들이 전체적인 맥을 짚었다면 구문식 접근은 보다 세세한 접근방법이 될 것이다.

1. 문장의 주어를 찾아라.

* The fact that his proposal makes sense/ should be avoided.
* The translation of the English novel/ will take me more than seven days.
* Putting an emotion into words and saying it out loud/ often helps.

2. 선행사를 수식하는 관계사절을 묶어라.

* The man (who had led me so surely through the forest) was blind.

3. 도치구문인지 파악한다.

* <u>His complaints</u> I cannot put up with any more.

4. 완료조동사의 의미를 정확히 파악한다.

* should have +p.p …했어야 했는데.
* cannot have +p.p …했을 리가 없다.
* must have +p.p …했음에 틀림없다.
* may have +p.p …했을지도 모른다.
* neednot have+p.p …할 필요가 없었는데.

5. 동사의 시제를 파악해라.

6. 진행시제, 완료시제, 수동태를 하나의 의미로 간주해라.

7. 문장의 기본 형식을 알면 긴 목적어도 잡을 수가 있다.
   I don't want to remember <u>feeling very frustrated and angry in my life.</u>

8. 명사 뒤의 전치사구, 분사, 부정사, 형용사적 수식어구는 괄호로 묶어라.(거품제거)

9. 평소에 다의어의 의미파악을 해라.

10. 공통된 어구를 찾아라.

11. 삽입구, 삽입절은 괄호로 묶어라.

12. 병렬구조를 파악해라.

13. 수와 시제일치에 주의해라.

14. 부정어가 문두에 나오면 도치구문을 생각해라.
   * **No** sooner **<u>had he met</u>** her than he ran away.

15. 동명사의 관용 어구를 학습해라.

V

Various English Reading

V Various English Reading

1 Suggestions from the Child Welfare League of America

- Volunteer your time. Get involved with other parents in your community. Help **vulnerable** children and their families. Start a **playgroup**.

- Discipline your children thoughtfully. Never discipline your child when you are upset. Give yourself time to calm down.

- Remember that discipline is a way to teach your child.

- Use privileges to encourage good behavior and time-outs to help your child regain control.

- Examine your behavior. Abuse is not just physical. Both words and actions can inflict deep, lasting wounds.

- Be a **nurturing** parent. Use your actions to show children and other adults that conflicts can be settled without hitting or yelling.

- Educate yourself and others. Simple support for children and parents can be the best way to prevent child abuse.

- After-school activities, parent education classes, mentoring programs, and **respite** care are some of the many ways to **keep** children safe **from** harm. Be a voice in support of these efforts in your community.

- Teach children their rights. When children are taught they are special and have the right to be safe, they are less likely to think abuse is their fault, and more likely to report an offender.

- Support prevention programs. Too often, intervention occurs only after abuse is reported.

- Greater investments are needed in programs that have been proven to stop the abuse before it occurs-such as family counseling and home visits by nurses who provide assistance for newborns and their parents.

- Know what child abuse is. Physical and sexual abuse clearly **constitute** maltreatment, but so does neglect, or the failure of parents or other caregivers to provide a child with needed food, clothing, and care.

- Children can also be emotionally abused when they are rejected, **berated**, or continuously isolated.

- Know the signs. Unexplained injuries aren't the only signs of abuse-depression.

- Fear of a certain adult, difficulty trusting others or making friends, sudden changes in eating or sleeping patterns, inappropriate sexual behavior, poor **hygiene**, secrecy, and hostility are often signs of family problems and may indicate a child is being neglected or physically, sexually, or emotionally abused.

Assignments

1. Look up the unfamiliar words.
2. Translate the above paragraph into Korean.
3. Memorize the useful expressions.

2 Introduction – What is Tourism?

Since the beginning of time humans have traveled. Food, water, safety or acquisition of resources (trade) were the early travel motivations. But the idea of travel for pleasure or exploration soon emerged. Travel has always depended upon technology to provide the means or **mode** of travel. The earliest travelers walked or rode **domesticated** animals. The invention of the wheel and the sail provided new modes of transportation. Each improvement in technology increased individuals' opportunities to travel. As roads were improved and governments **stabilized**, interest in travel increased for education, sightseeing, and religious purposes. One of the earliest travel guides was written by Pausanias, a Greek, which was a 10 volume Guide to Greece, for Roman tourists in 170 A.D..

Tourism is a collection of activities, services and industries that delivers a travel experience, including transportation, accommodations, eating and drinking establishments, retail shops, entertainment businesses, activity facilities and other hospitality services provided for individuals or groups traveling away from home. The World Tourism Organization (WTO) claims that tourism is currently the worlds largest industry with annual **revenues** of over $3 trillion dollars. Tourism provides over six million jobs in the United States, making it the country's largest **employer**.

Assignments

1. Look up the unfamiliar words.
2. Translate the above paragraph into Korean.
3. Memorize the useful expressions.

3 Our sweet home

My stepdaughter is 22 years old and still living at home, although she stays with her boyfriend several nights a week at his sister's apartment. Last week she came home to take a shower and dress for church. Her boyfriend stayed in her bedroom while she changed clothes. I am very uncomfortable with this **behavior** at our home.

I know she sleeps with him at his sister's place. I feel like a **hypocrite** going to church and not **stand**ing **up for** what I believe in my own home. I have repeatedly asked her father to talk to her about having boyfriends in her bedroom, but he will not say anything. Since this is his adult child, do I have any **authority** to **demand** that she not have men in her room? After all, this is my house, too. I really want to approach this

properly. Can you help? -Not comfortable

You are in a **tough spot**. You can ask your stepdaughter not to bring men into her bedroom, but if her father says it's OK, you are out of luck. We suggest you talk to your husband and see if you can get him **on the same page**. Then you can tell her, "Your father and I would appreciate it if you wouldn't bring your boyfriend into your bedroom." Make sure he backs you up.

Assignments

1. Look up the unfamiliar words.
2. Translate the above paragraph into Korean.
3. Memorize the useful expressions.

4 Why Having Kids Is Bad for Your Health

It's unfortunate, but true : parenting may be hazardous to your health, at least according to new research that shows that mothers consume more calories and get less physical activity than women with no kids.

In the latest **knock** against **parenthood**, researchers from the University of Minnesota looked at 838 women and 682 men and concluded that having children — particularly for moms

— is linked to an **array** of negative outcomes. Mothers had a higher **body-mass index** and didn't eat as healthily as childless women, chugging more sugary drinks and eating more total calories and saturated fat.

Both moms and dads exercised less than their child-free counterparts, but in a completely unfair twist, fathers' BMI didn't differ from that of men without children.

Parents are more apt to not take good care of their health at a time when they really need to be modeling healthy behavior for their miniature **doppelgangers**. That, of course, is easier said than done. The pressures of parenting are **relentless**, and sometimes it's easier to stick a frozen pizza in the microwave than **fuss with coax**ing kids to whole grains and leafy greens.

"All parents can relate to the idea of demands and **trade-offs**," says Jerica Berge, lead researcher and an assistant professor in the Department of Family Medicine and Community Health at the University of Minnesota. She's also the mother of a 2-year-old and 6-year-old. "We've all felt that we want to cook a healthy meal, but we've got to get out of here to make that appointment. We all relate to that feeling of not being able to pay attention to your health because of parenting demands."

In the study, published online Monday in the journal **Pediatrics**, moms got less exercise per week, 4.5 hours of physical activity compared with the 6 hours that non-mothers got. The American Heart Association recommends 30 minutes of exercise per day most days of the week.

Mothers also ate more calories, 2,360 compared with childless women's 1,992. "The difference between those is significant", says Berge. The research didn't focus on what the difference might be attributed to, but Berge didn't disagree when this reporter suggested those 368 calories could easily result from grazing on children's **leftovers**.

Researchers found that mothers and non-mothers ate similar quantities of nutritious foods — whole grains, fruits, vegetables — but moms also ate more unhealthy foods. "We think moms, though trying to model by eating fruits and vegetables, might be having a conflict with time demands so instead of opting to cook a healthy meal, they're making chicken **nuggets** and macaroni and cheese", says Berge. "They're probably eating them with their kids too, so they are eating high-fat foods at the same time they're eating healthy foods, and it kind of

undoes the healthy foods."

From a public-health perspective, Berge says it's critical to **intervene** so that the behavior is not **perpetuated** from generation to generation.

Pediatricians, for example, address a child's dietary intake at well-child visits; that might be a good time to ask about the family's eating habits, too. If everyone's dining daily on pizza and corn dogs, the pediatrician might offer a gentle reality chcck.

If time is the problem, involve the kids, **coercing** thcm to set the table and getting them involved in the **prep work**. Figure out how to serve healthy foods quickly; putting baby carrots and dip on a plate takes no more time than setting out chips.

What constitutes physical activity may also need some rethinking. It doesn't just have to be working the **elliptical** at the gym. Moms, don't sit on the bench at the park; kick a ball around with your kids. Choose stairs over elevators. Walk to school. "Incorporate physical activity into time with your kids because it's probably not going to happen on its own", says Berge.

Assignments

1. Look up the unfamiliar words.
2. Translate the above paragraph into Korean.
3. Memorize the useful expressions.

5 Shutting him away

My father married my stepmother 20 years ago. Three years ago, he suffered a **stroke**. Though moderately disabled, he is still mentally sharp, didn't lose speech and is able to do most things for himself.

He is happy as a **homebody**, but my stepmother has made it increasingly clear that he will be going off to **a care facility** soon. Dad has **reluctantly** agreed. The problem is, the place she's chosen is nowhere near any family members. She claims she will visit him often, but we know she is planning to do more travelling, and my father will be left completely isolated. She refuses to consider a closer alternative and shuts anyone down who mentions it. Dad is afraid to speak up. We are all **heartbroken**. What can we do? -Need to Protect Dad

Is this possibly a financial issue? Is the chosen facility less expensive than one near you? Could you contribute to the cost? Otherwise, if your stepmother is deliberately isolating Dad, it could be considered elder abuse. Explain the problem to Dad's doctor and ask for assistance. You also can contact the local Adult Protective Services or get information through the Eldercare Locator and the National Center on Elder Abuse.

Assignments

1. Look up the unfamiliar words.
2. Translate the above paragraph into Korean.
3. Memorize the useful expressions.

6 Husband who lied

I am 26 and have been living with my "husband" for a year. We had a religious ceremony, but didn't file the legal **paperwork**. Now I realize it was a huge mistake. I desperately want out of this so-called marriage.

"Justin" lied about completing his college education and was unemployed for the first six months we were together. He told me he was applying for jobs, but in reality, he spent his days playing video games and eating junk food. Justin finally found part-time minimum-wage employment, but I still do the cleaning, bill-paying and cooking despite working 50 hours a week compared to his 20. I have asked, begged and nagged him to help more, but he refuses to lift a finger. When I insist, he whines and takes an hour to do a 20-minute task.

Justin suffers from depression. Whenever I bring up the idea of an **amicable** separation, he either becomes **enraged** and throws the furniture, or dissolves into a sobbing mess and threatens suicide. I, too, have fought and won my own battle with depression through therapy, medication and a wonderful support network. I feel the need to provide a stable environment for Justin, but he refuses to seek treatment.

If I leave him, I am terrified he will harm himself. Justin's Parents are less than sympathetic, and he cannot support himself. I have moved into the second bedroom, and we haven't had sex for months. Justin insists we are married and everything is fine. Our friends and family have no clue that it's not legal and our relationship is in **shambles**. A messy breakup could cost me my career. Please help. -Cornered in Kansas

As much as you want to help Justin, you are not responsible for his mental health or his unwillingness to seek treatment. At some point, his dependence is self-destructive to both of you. You could tell him you will consider staying if he gets therapy immediately. But also talk to your local clergy person about your "marriage". Kansas recognizes common-law marriages, and you could, in fact, be legally bound to Justin. If walking out is not possible, you may need to file the legal paperwork and then get an actual divorce or have the marriage **annul**led.

Assignments

1. Look up the unfamiliar words.
2. Translate the above paragraph into Korean.
3. Memorize the useful expressions.

7 Inconsiderate hubbie

I am a divorced mother of two colledge-age girls. Over the years, their father hasn't bothered to have much contact with them.

The problem is, in the past two years, we have received a picture at Christmas of his four little girls by his second wife. This really hurts my daughters' feelings and just makes me mad. It's like he is throwing his new family in our faces. It even says "Merry Christmas from the family". Do you think this is right? **-Disgusted** in Penn.

It is extremely insensitive, but we don't believe Dad is trying to deliberately hurtful. And his wife is likely the one who is doing a mass mailing without considering the recipients. Let your ex know that you appreciate his effort to stay in touch with his children, but ask that he please not send the photograph because it makes them terribly unhappy. We hope he cares enough to do something about it.

Assignments

1. Look up the unfamiliar words.
2. Translate the above paragraph into Korean.
3. Memorize the useful expressions.

8 Mommy trouble

I've been married eight years, and the entire time there have been problems between my mother and my husband. I'm used to my mother's rude, **disrespectful** ways, but my husband is not.

To avoid constant criticism and **bickering**, we limit our contact with her. Mom complained about this, and I politely explained why she sees less of us. Of course, this didn't help because she sees nothing wrong with her behavior. She said my husband made me say these things and he's the one keeping us away from her. She refuses to see it's her own doing.

I've learned that Mom **has cried to** the rest of my family about how horrible my husband it, never missing an opportunity to **badmouth** him. I don't see the rest of my family very often, and I hate to think they believe my mom. She can be very **convincing**. My main concern is that she'll talk that way around my 6-year-old daughter, and I don't think that would be good.

It's a shame that honest discussion has never helped and avoiding her is what works best. Should I suggest she talk to a therapist, or are some people just naturally unpleasant to be around? -Midwest Mess

You could ask your mother to go to therapy with you, together, to work on your problems. Still, it will help to keep in touch with the rest of the family so they can get to know your husband the way you do. And if Mom sys one negative thing about your husband to his child, you should remove the girl from her presence and inform Mom that there will be no more visits with her granddaughter unless she can behave.

Assignments

1. Look up the unfamiliar words.
2. Translate the above paragraph into Korean.
3. Memorize the useful expressions.

9 Filthy friend

My husband and I have a single male friend who built a beautiful home four years ago. He'd behave us over for a barbecue at his new place once or twice a year. Lately, though, it appears he has not cleaned the house since he first moved in.

"Matt" has two dogs and there is dog hair everywhere. The rugs look like they have never been vacuumed. The kitchen **countertops** look dirty and I don't even want to discuss the bathrooms.

My husband and I have started making excuses not to visit and especially no to eat in his home. Matt live in a remote area and cleaning help may be hard to find, but my husband would like to suggest he hire someone to do his housekeeping. Do you have any way to help us get this point across to Matt without hurting his feelings? -Matt's Friends

Men are generally less sensitive about issues of housekeeping than woman are. Next time you visit, we don't think Matt would be overly embarrassed if you simply said, "Matt, you ought to get someone in here to help you clean up. Dogs shed a lot." It would be even better if you had a name to give him. Do a little online research and see if there is a cleaning service in the area. Or suggest Matt ask one of his neighbors if they know anyone. You'd be doing him a favor.

Assignments

1. Look up the unfamiliar words.
2. Translate the above paragraph into Korean.
3. Memorize the useful expressions.

10 Stressed out? Wondering what to do?

It does happen. Caring for children is sometimes a difficult task. Discipline is especially **challenging**.

Here are some ideas that can help :

Talk about feelings. Take your child's feelings seriously and work through them.

Use firm communication. Say what you mean, and mean what you say.

Model the behavior that you desire in them. Children learn from what they see and hear.

Encourage your children often and **recognize** each one's personal best.

Use "time-out" balanced with "time-in". Remember, discipline is a verb meaning "to teach".

Assignments

1. Look up the unfamiliar words.
2. Translate the above paragraph into Korean.
3. Memorize the useful expressions.

11 More than blood ties

This is in response to "To Gift or Not To Gift", whose daughter-in-law was talking about a divorce. "Gift" wanted to know if the daughter-in-law should be taken off the annual gift list. It is always best to take the peaceful way in a family matter. I did and never **regret**ted it. When my son and his wife split up, I told them both that I love them and their child and would not make my granddaughter choose between her parents. I included my daughter-in-law in all **family gatherings**.

They separated, but never divorced. When my son was killed a few months later, I said as far as I was concerned there was no separation. I included my daughter-in-law in planning the funeral and the **obituary**. People **had the nerve to** say I shouldn't have been so **inclusive**, but I told them I was the mother and this is what I wanted. I did it for my daughter-in-law, my granddaughter and our family. We are still close, and my granddaughter stays with me quite a bit. Had I made enemies with my daughter-in-law when they separated, I may not have had the chance to spend so much time with my son's daughter. I say give her the gift. and the next time she complains about your son, simply say. "You're talking about my child, and it hurts me to hear negative things about him. Please don't put me n the middle like that." You will be surprised how fast she will respect your wishes.

My daughter-in-law once asked whether I minded if she still considered me to be her mother-in-law, even if she someday remarries. I told her I would be honored. -A.G.

You did it right. Brava.

Assignments

1. Look up the unfamiliar words.
2. Translate the above paragraph into Korean.
3. Memorize the useful expressions.

12 Caught in the middle

I have the sinking feeling that my parents, who have been married for 20years, don't love each other anymore. Moa and Dad are always insulting each other. They never give **compliments** or even say I love you, except on special occasions. Sometimes I think the only reason they are together is my brother and I.

I am only 11 years old and can already pick up on their **disconnection**. The main thing I'm worried about is divorce and making me **pick sides**. They are very nice to my brother and me, but not to each other. Last week, Dad called my mom and my brother some not-very-nice-names, and they stormed out of the house and didn't come home until really late.

When my parents fight, I feel terrible. I just want to jump out the window. Don't even suggest counseling. I already did and they laughed and said they don't need it. I showed them an entry in my journal about my feelings and they said I'm too young to feel this way. I'm so confused.

I just want to relax for the rest of the summer, but I feel I **have an elephant on my shoulders**. -Confused and Frustrated

Not all arguing leads to divorce, but even so, it's obvious your parents don't realize how upsetting this is for you. You need an **advocate**. Discuss your concerns with a grandparent, favorite relative, your clergy person or a school counselor, and ask one of them to talk to your folks about what's going on. We hope it will help.

Assignments

1. Look up the unfamiliar words.
2. Translate the above paragraph into Korean.
3. Memorize the useful expressions.

13 Accused husband

A good friend asked if anyone would be willing to lend their home to host a surprise 30th birthday party for his wife and said he would **compensate** them. I happily volunteered.

My wife insisted I could not accept any compensation, so I told my friend the party was our gift to his wife. The party turned out great, but this morning my friend stopped by with a thank-you note and a check for $100.

My wife says I can't cash it, it's not proper etiquette, I'm cheap, etc. I say if I made it clear we didn't expect anything, but he still chose to compensate us, we should accept it. I think he'd be offended if we were to give it back. What is proper? -Accused of Being Cheap

It is OK to accept compensation. However, if your wife **disagree**s and you think your friend will be offended if you return the check, donate it to charity in the birthday girl's name.

Assignments

1. Look up the unfamiliar words.
2. Translate the above paragraph into Korean.
3. Memorize the useful expressions.

14 Fashion that satisfies everyone

I am tired of **midriff** shirts and low-rise jeans that are super-tight. These clothes are **offensive** when they are on young girls. It shows the world way too much skin. We are parents of a **preteen**, and we are constantly battling to find appropriate clothes for her age and already **mature** body shape. Please help us bring in fashion that meets the standards of both parents and children. -V.

You are **preach**ing to the choir. The good news is, fashion changes. Low-rise jeans and midriff tops are already on the way out. We've printed letters on this subject before, and readers suggested purchasing athletic wear or **patronizing** stores like Old Navy and Lands' End, which carry appropriate trendy clothing in all sizes. You also should talk to the managers of the stores where you shop and ask them to stock styles that appeal to parents of young girls, as well as their daughters.

Assignments

1. Look up the unfamiliar words.
2. Translate the above paragraph into Korean.
3. Memorize the useful expressions.

15 Easy Disciplining

"Stop that crying, or I'll give you something to cry about!"

If you heard this as a child, you're not alone. What was once seen as an acceptable way to speak to a child has, fortunately, fallen **out of fashion**.

But there are those days. **Cranky** kids who will be satisfied by nothing. Children acting "spoiled". Kids pushing the limits of what they can **get away with**. Whether the child is 2 or 15 doesn't matter. It's frustrating, even anger-provoking, for a parent.

There are answers, and they don't involve special education or hours of learning. Once put in place, they have a double bonus : they make parenting easier. These ideas are not in a particular order; they all work together.

Take care of yourself. A parent who is healthy and at least relatively happy is a better parent. If you aren't in that situation, that's no excuse to treat the child differently, but take a look at which measures you can take to enjoy your life more. This will help you be more patient and loving when dealing with discipline.

Understand the environment. Children are much more likely to be cranky in certain situations : very hot/cold weather, a stressful day at school/daycare, on vacation, when there is family tension, when bored, hungry, thirsty, etc.; and anytime their normal routine is **altered**. This does not excuse any form of behavior, but put your discipline in context. If you've been at the mall all day, your young child probably does feel like **squalling**. Don't we all sometimes?

Give clear, consistent expectations and consequences. If a child "**gets away with murder**" at a family reunion and then is whipped for speaking up at the dinner table, he will grow up confused and distrusting of adults-and, if **spanked**, is shown by research to be more likely to be violent himself as an adult. Set clear, fair guidelines. Explain them in a way each child will understand. Tell them the consequences, and **enforce** them. If you're having difficulty enforcing them, it might be because you aren't **consistent** or that the consequences are too harsh.

Assignments

1. Look up the unfamiliar words.
2. Translate the above paragraph into Korean.
3. Memorize the useful expressions.

16 Tobacco-Free Kids

Tobacco use is the No. 1 cause of **preventable** death in America, yet tobacco products are **exempt** from basic health regulations that apply to other products we consume, such as food and drugs. As a teen and especially as a girl, I am continuously targeted by the tobacco companies.

In the past two years, the industry has launched an **aggressive** marketing campaign to depict cigarette smoking as feminine and fashionable, rather than the harmful and deadly **addiction** it is. Cigarettes are now packed to look like perfume and as things called "purse packs".

Considering lung cancer is the leading cancer killer of women, these cigarettes are putting the health of girls like my friends and me at risk. I have never been one to just sit around and complain, so I joined the Campaign for Tobacco-Free Kids as a youth advocate leading the fight to reduce tobacco use and its devastating consequences.

The campaign is working to change public attitudes and policies on tobacco, prevent kids from smoking, and help young smokers to quit. Your readers can get involved by visiting tobaccofreekids. org and learning more about FDA legislation that would regulate the manufacturing, marketing and sale of tobacco products.

They can also learn about how they can raise awareness about tobacco-related disease prevention. Thanks for your help spreading the word. It's time to show tobacco companies they can't target women and kids anymore. -Auriel, age 17, Fla.

We appreciate your wise words and the helpful information. It's a great website and we hope our young readers will take a look.

Assignments

1. Look up the unfamiliar words.
2. Translate the above paragraph into Korean.
3. Memorize the useful expressions.

17 Cradle robber

I've been dating "Hannah" for three months. It hasn't been easy because my parents don't **approve of** her, even as a friend, because she's 19 and I'm 15. Until now, we've been great together. We talked at least three times a day, hardly ever fought, and just had a great relationship. But my parents have

tightened **up** and officially **suspend**ed me from seeing her. Mom refuses to back down. I told Hannah, and now she tells me she can't handle the distance between us and thinks we should break up. It makes me so mad because just the other day she was talking about how much she was in love with me.

Am I tying her down? Should I break up with her so she can be free? I'm sure she misses being able to **flirt with** anyone she wants. A 15-year-old is probably holding her back, right? -Ball and Chain

You sound pretty **levelheaded** for a 15-year-old, so we'll be straight with you. Hannah needs to spread her wings a bit and, more importantly, so do you. She is probably your first significant girlfriend, but everyone should have the opportunity to do some **comparison shopping** before settling down.

At 19, Hannah is ready for things you shouldn't have to think about for a few years, and it's unfair to both of you to be in a serious relationship at this stage. And if the relationship includes sex, there are laws that could get Hannah into serious trouble. If, in a few years, you'd like to reconnect, by all means give it a go.

Assignments

1. Look up the unfamiliar words.
2. Translate the above paragraph into Korean.
3. Memorize the useful expressions.

18 Her cheatin' heart

I am a 36-year-old husband and father, married for four years. Two years ago, I caught my wife cheating on me. I was willing to forgive her for the sake of our children. But lately, our marriage seems to have fallen into that dark **alley** again. My wife is always on Facebook or buried in her cell phone, texting. She won't tell me with whom. Every time I dare peek at what she is doing, she goes immediately on the **defensive**.

I confronted her about how **shady** she had been, and she assures me it's nothing to be concerned about. Well, time, aggravation and arguments have turned me into someone I don't like. I logged into her Facebook account and checked out her private messages. I discovered she's been talking to some guy behind my back. It's not an affair, but there is definite flirting. I haven't told her what I know. Should I? Was I wrong to **snoop**? Help. -Distrustful

Although we don't **recommend** snooping, it is understandable when your wife has given you reason to suspect her and has a history to back it up. Tell her what you found, and apologize for going behind her back. When someone has had an affair, that person needs to be completely **transparent** in every aspect of the relationship, or trust cannot be regained. Your wife is putting your marriage at risk by being dishonest about her contact with other men. Insist that she accompany you for counseling, and see if you can work on this together.

Assignments

1. Look up the unfamiliar words.
2. Translate the above paragraph into Korean.
3. Memorize the useful expressions.

19 For the sake of our baby

My husband and I have large breed dogs. Four of them are well behave and nice to be around. The fifth is a nightmare. "Buddy" constantly **attack**s our other dogs and has caused minor injuries. I have spoken to three different trainers and have tried every thing. I want to have Buddy relocated to another home. He is not a bad dog. He just doesn't fit into our pack.

My husband has only recently **decide**d to take this seriously and is now determined to keep this dog. But last night, Buddy attacked our St. Bernard, and in the process, I was knocked over and bitten. I'm done.

We are expecting our first child soon, and Buddy is clearly a risk. How do I convince my husband of this without getting divorced? -Illinois

Even **well-behaved** dogs can develop jealousy toward a new baby. Although Buddy may be trainable, it's unlikely you will **accomplish** that before the baby arrives, and your child's safety must come first. Your husband is doing Buddy no favors by insisting he fit in with your family when he might do better and be happier elsewhere. **Don't wait for a tragedy**. Please relocate Buddy immediately.

Assignments

1. Look up the unfamiliar words.
2. Translate the above paragraph into Korean.
3. Memorize the useful expressions.

20 Not Daddy's girl

My father has a habit of touching me when he talks. He'll tap my hand or leg, and he often touches my arm when it's unnecessary. I've told him many times that I don't like it, but he gets quite unhappy if I ask him to stop. IIe's donc this since I was a kid, and I'm 33 now.

Once, when I was 13, he kept tapping his leg against mine under the table at an outdoor restaurant. I couldn't tolerate it and moved my leg away. My father flew into a **rage**, **snarl**ing and **grit**ting his teeth and telling me I had a "disgusting habit".

I am going to my parents' house tomorrow and am not looking forward to it. I have to remember not to sit near Dad and to stand at least two feet away when he speaks to me. The problem is that while he's talking, he moves closer and then starts tapping me. It infuriates me that he won't stop no matter how many times I've asked him to.

Here's what I suspect : My father considers me his property. He wants to be able to put his hands on me the way one does with a pet. When I ask him to stop, he is insulted as if his property is being taken from him. I also suspect he taps me because he thinks I'm not listening and needs to keep my attention.

I avoid my parents as much as possible and don't speak to my father unless it is absolutely necessary. Do other readers have this problem? -Son who is Wondering.

It is common for parents to touch their children when speaking to them. In most instances, it is a sign of affection. We can understand, however, how constant tapping could be annoying, although your reaction seems **out of proportion**. If Dad is tapping your arm to keep your attention from drifting, you can work on getting him to stop, but it requires that you **put a lid on** your level of hostility. Try talking to him, saying that you love him but it makes you extremely uncomfortable to be touched constantly. Remind him gently when he starts up.

Assignments

1. Look up the unfamiliar words.
2. Translate the above paragraph into Korean.
3. Memorize the useful expressions.

21 Big age gap

What are your views on older women dating younger men? I am 56, and he is 36. He first asked me to marry him 10 years ago, but I broke it off, thinking I was doing him a favor.

I then married someone else, hoping he would find someone his age. He did, but that marriage didn't last. Neither did mine. Am I being selfish? Is their any possibility that we could be happy together? My family has given us their **blessing**, but his is another story. I love him enough to let him go if you think I should. -Happy but Older

The only question is whether or not he wants **biological children**. No marriage is a sure thing. Yours doesn't come with fewer guarantees than any other. Our best wished and congratulations.

Assignments

1. Look up the unfamiliar words.
2. Translate the above paragraph into Korean.
3. Memorize the useful expressions.

22 Hooked on Addiction : From Food to Drugs to Internet Porn

America is having an addiction moment. Media headlines scream daily about new **neuroscience** findings on porn addiction, Internet addiction, food addiction and plain, old-fashioned drug addiction. As TIME's Michael Scherer wrote last week, 42 U.S.

Senators called on Attorney General Eric Holder to increase **obscenity prosecutions** for pornography, due in part to fears over sex addiction. There's even a new online magazine about addiction called The Fix.

But what do the recent neuroscience studies actually tell us about addiction? What is addiction really? An article on the website referenced by the U.S. Senators in their letter to Holder explained sex addiction this way :

Cocaine, **opioids**, alcohol, and other drugs **subvert**, or hijack, [the brain's] pleasure systems, and cause the brain to think a drug high is necessary to survive. Evidence is now strong that natural rewards such as food and sex affect the reward systems in the same way drugs affect them, thus the current interest in 'natural addiction'. Addiction, whether to cocaine, food, or sex occurs when these activities cease to contribute to a state of **homeostasis**, and instead cause adverse consequences.

But this is actually a **bizarre** form of circular reasoning. For one thing, it confuses the original purpose of the brain's pleasure **pathways**. If you think about it, these regions aren't very likely to have evolved specifically to enable us to get high on cocaine or heroin — that would be evolutionary **sabotage**.

But they almost certainly did evolve to get us to pursue food and sex relentlessly, in order to guarantee our survival. So, these brain regions are designed to make food and sex fun.

Suggesting that drugs "hijack" these reward systems to produce addiction implies that under normal circumstances — in the pursuit of "healthy" urges like eating and sex — these systems wouldn't cause addiction. Except of course the same reasoning, turned around, is used to argue that in fact food and sex are addictions — because they activate the brain regions that generate pleasure from drugs.

All that can actually be said based on this data is that food, sex, drugs — and anything else that's fun — activate brain regions and cause pleasure, and that people enjoy and pursue pleasure. However, that does little to explain why said brain activity can sometimes cause addiction, but mostly doesn't. The vast majority of people aren't food or drug addicts — and it's not clear what's different about the minority who are.

So pleasure alone isn't addiction — and not even craving plus pleasure are enough to define addiction. The most accepted definition, as implied by the link above, describes addiction as **compulsive** behavior related to a substance or activity that people continue to engage in despite negative consequences. That's the essence of the definition used by the DSM, **psychiatry**'s diagnostic manual.

It's a complex phenomenon that goes beyond mere activation of pleasure pathways. Unfortunately, most animal and brain-imaging studies tell us very little about it. Last week, for example, I reported on a study about "food addiction": researchers found that when women were presented with a chocolate milkshake, those who had more symptoms of food addiction had greater activity in brain regions linked with pleasure and **craving**, and reduced activity in areas connected with self-control, compared with those who had few or no food-addiction symptoms.

That's interesting, but again all it really shows is that symptomatic participants predictably reported more pleasure and craving, and less self-control. And it's important to note that none of the women in the study actually had food addiction; some had symptoms, but none had **full-fledged** eating disorders. The brain differences shown in the study, therefore, were seen in perfectly normal people — most of whom, prior research suggests, will never be addicted to food.

No study has ever isolated a simple brain change that is always seen in addicts and never in non-addicts. And although some studies have found changes that can help predict an addict's odds of **relapse**, they're not always accurate.

This failure to define or understand the **blurry** line between the normal and the **pathological** leads to all kinds of misconceptions about addiction : for example, thinking that simple exposure to a substance or experience is enough to create addiction. Most of us enjoy the occasional chocolate milkshake, but virtually none of us would rob a bank to get one if the price became **unaffordable**. Similarly, more than 97% of people who take opioid painkillers like Oxycontin as prescribed, and don't have a prior history of addiction, do not become addicted, studies show.

And as Virginia Heffernan pointed out in the New York Times this week, college students who define themselves as "Internet addicts" don't actually behave very differently than their predecessors who were also occasionally known to **blow off** homework and stay up late in pursuit of a hobby or interest.

Addiction research is continually filling in parts of the puzzle of addictive behavior. But to use existing evidence to claim that sex and food create overpowering drives by "hijacking" the brain's pleasure pathways doesn't tell the whole story. We need to understand a lot more about how we control and choose our behavior ordinarily before we can truly know what causes our decisions to go awry in addiction. If we don't understand how food and sex normally affect our brains and our choices, how can we understand what triggers addictions to any substance or experience?

Assignments

1. Look up the unfamiliar words.
2. Translate the above paragraph into Korean.
3. Memorize the useful expressions.

23 When Mom Exercises in Pregnancy, Her Baby's Heart Benefits

One of the great things about pregnancy is that it offers a seemingly **plausible** excuse to **indulge** — eat a little more dessert (why not, when you're going to gain so much weight anyway) and dial down that hard-core exercise **regimen** (see first parenthetical). But new research **upends** that **mindset**, showing that exercise during pregnancy can actually result in a healthier baby.

That exercising while pregnant is good for mom is hardly

news, but now that mothers-to-be know it's good for their babies, it will be that much harder to **morph** into a couch potato. Maternal **guilt** can now rear its head months before baby even appears on the scene, prompting Mom to hit the treadmill, hard.

Previous research has indicated that exercise in the first **trimester**, when the placenta is formed, helps forge extra blood vessels so that there is more opportunity to exchange nutrients between mom and baby.

Linda May, an exercise physiologist and **anatomist** at Kansas City University of Medicine and Biosciences, figured there were bound to be sustained benefits for the baby too.

May and colleagues collected **noninvasive fetal** heart measurements from 66 fetuses when their mothers reached 28, 32 and 36 weeks of a typical 40-week pregnancy. Some of the mothers engaged in moderate to vigorous aerobic activity for 30 minutes at least three times a week; others didn't exercise.

Researchers then assessed fetal heart rate and heart rate variability, which is the span between beats. Heart rate variability is indicative of heart health, which is associated with better overall health : people with increased variability are exercisers, and their hearts function more efficiently; those with decreased variability may be **cardiac** patients or, at the least, couch potatoes.

At 32 weeks, researchers started to see changes in heart response in the fetuses of the exercising moms. By 36 weeks, they noted what May calls a "big, significant change" — lower heart rate and increased heart rate variability.

When researchers analyzed the frequency with which Mom exercised, they found that the more activity, the lower the fetal heart rate and the higher the heart rate variability. "If she just does a little bit, it will have benefit," says May. "If she does more, it will help more. It's similar to the exercise response of an adult. It's very cool."

Even cooler is the way the results continued to manifest themselves after birth. Some women dropped out of the research due to **attrition**, but 43 moms brought their babies back when they were 1 month old. Their hearts still showed that pumped-up quality, according to the study, which **is slated for** publication in the journal Early Human Development.

"It suggests the result we saw was real, and that it is giving this baby a healthier heart," says May.

Assignments

1. Look up the unfamiliar words.
2. Translate the above paragraph into Korean.
3. Memorize the useful expressions.

24 Can't Get Enough Coffee? It Might Be in Your Genes

If you rely on a deep, **sludgy** kick of java to get you through the day, your need for caffeine might have something to do with your genes : a team of researchers have identified variations on two genes that may influence how much coffee people consume.

The study was a meta-analysis of data from five studies involving 47,341 U.S. participants of European **descent**, and run by scientists from the National Cancer Institute, Harvard School of Public Health, Brigham and Women's Hospital, and the University of North Carolina at Chapel Hill.

The genes in question are known as CYP1A2, which is involved with the body's caffeine metabolism, and AHR, which regulates CYP1A2. Scientists found that people with high-consumption **variants** of either gene on both **chromosomes** consumed on average about 40 mg more caffeine per day than people who didn't have the **mutation** on either chromosome.

Forty milligrams is not a huge amount, equivalent to a can of soda or a third of a cup of coffee. The researchers measured all sources from which participants got caffeine, including soda, tea and chocolate, but about 80% came from coffee.

The authors acknowledge that the influence of these genes on caffeine intake is small, accounting for less than 1% of the variation in coffee consumption in the reviewed studies. But the results suggest that there may be many other genes that **contribute to** how much caffeine people consume, and may help researchers better understand the effects of the drug on the body.

The Boston Globe's Daily Dose blog reported :

What's interesting, though, is that mutations studied were involved with how fast the body metabolizes caffeine as well as certain chemicals and **toxic** substances. And it could be that those who metabolize caffeine faster are more likely to be looking quickly for their next hit of coffee than those who are slow metabolizers, [study co-author and professor of computational biology at Brigham and Women's Hospital Daniel] Chasman speculates.

And — if you want to take these theories one step beyond

— these gene mutations that **predispose** some to a higher caffeine intake might also protect them from dangerous toxins by flushing them more quickly out of the body. And that could provide some explanation for why coffee drinkers have been found in the latest research to have fewer health problems like strokes.

Assignments

1. Look up the unfamiliar words.
2. Translate the above paragraph into Korean.
3. Memorize the useful expressions.

25 Why Exercise Won't Make You Thin

As I write this, tomorrow is Tuesday, which is a **cardio** day. I'll spend five minutes warming up on the VersaClimber, a **towering** machine that requires you to move your arms and legs simultaneously. Then I'll do 30 minutes on a stair mill. On Wednesday a personal trainer will work me like a farm animal for an hour, sometimes to the point that I am dizzy — an abuse for which I pay as much as I spend on groceries in a week. Thursday is "body **wedge**" class, which involves another exercise **contraption**, this one a large foam wedge from which I will push myself up in various hateful ways for an hour. Friday will bring a 5.5-mile run, the extra half-mile my grueling **expiation** of any **gastronomical** indulgences during the week.

I have exercised like this — obsessively, a bit **grimly** — for years, but recently I began to wonder : Why am I doing this? Except for a two-year period at the end of an unhappy relationship — a period when I self-medicated with lots of Italian desserts — I have never been overweight. One of the most widely accepted, commonly repeated assumptions in our culture is that if you exercise, you will lose weight. But I exercise all the time, and since I ended that relationship and cut most of those desserts, my weight has returned to the same 163 lb. It has been most of my adult life. I still have **gut** fat that hangs over my belt when I sit. Why isn't all the exercise wiping it out?

It's a question many of us could ask. More than 45 million Americans now belong to a health club, up from 23 million in 1993. We spend some $19 billion a year on gym memberships. Of course, some people join and never go. Still, as one major study — the Minnesota Heart Survey — found, more of us at least say we exercise regularly. The survey ran from 1980, when only 47% of respondents said they engaged in regular exercise, to 2000, when the figure had grown to 57%.

And yet **obesity** figures have risen dramatically in the same period : a third of Americans are obese, and another third count as overweight by the Federal Government's definition. Yes, it's entirely possible that those of us who regularly go to the gym would weigh even more if we exercised less. But like many other people, I get hungry after I exercise, so I often eat more on the days I work out than on the days I don't. Could exercise actually be keeping me from losing weight?

The conventional wisdom that exercise is essential for **shedding** pounds is actually fairly new. As recently as the 1960s, doctors routinely advised against rigorous exercise, particularly for older adults who could injure themselves. Today doctors encourage even their oldest patients to exercise, which is sound advice for many reasons : People who regularly exercise are at significantly lower risk for all manner of diseases — those of the heart in particular. They less often develop cancer, diabetes and many other illnesses. But the past few years of obesity research show that the role of exercise in weight loss has been wildly overstated.

"In general, for weight loss, exercise is pretty useless", says

Eric Ravussin, chair in diabetes and metabolism at Louisiana State University and a prominent exercise researcher. Many recent studies have found that exercise isn't as important in helping people lose weight as you hear so regularly in gym advertisements or on shows like The Biggest Loser — or, for that matter, from magazines like this one.

The basic problem is that while it's true that exercise burns calories and that you must burn calories to lose weight, exercise has another effect : it can stimulate hunger. That causes us to eat more, which in turn can **negate** the weight-loss benefits we just **accrue**d. Exercise, in other words, isn't necessarily helping us lose weight. It may even be making it harder.

Assignments

1. Look up the unfamiliar words.
2. Translate the above paragraph into Korean.
3. Memorize the useful expressions.

26 An Apple a Day Keeps Cholesterol at Bay?

Lending **credence** to the old **adage** about eating an apple a day, a new study finds that women who ate the fruit daily saw improvements in cholesterol levels and markers of **inflammation**

— suggesting a lower risk of heart disease — in a year's time. The study, conducted by researchers at Florida State University, involved 160 women who were randomly assigned to eat about 2.7 ounces (75g) of dried apples or prunes (dried plums) daily. Researchers did blood tests at the three-, six- and 12-month marks to measure heart-risk factors.

After a year, the women who ate dried apples had lowered their total cholesterol by 14%; their levels of LDL (or "bad") cholesterol had fallen by 23%, and their levels of HDL (or good) cholesterol had increased by about 4%. Participants also experienced a 32% decline in C-reactive protein, an indicator of inflammation in the body and a risk factor for heart disease.

The women who ate prunes saw also slight reductions in these risk factors, but not to the same extent as those who ate apples, said study author and professor of nutrition Bahram H. Arjmandi.

As an extra benefit, the women in apple group lost about 3.3 lbs. on average — even though the dried fruit added an extra 240 calories to their diets.

Researchers chose to study apples in human volunteers, because previous data from animal studies had suggested health benefits. Reported WebMD :

Apples are rich in pectin, a soluble fiber, which blocks cholesterol absorption in the gut and encourages the body to use, rather than store, the waxy stuff. Apple peels are also packed with polyphenols — antioxidants that prevent cellular damage from free radicals.

Though the study used dried apples for convenience, Arjmandi says fresh are likely to be even better. And it doesn't matter if they're green, red, or golden. "Any varieties of apples are good", he says.

Another key, [University of California, Davis, nutritionist Dianne] Hyson says, is eating the whole fruit, rather than looking for individual components in supplements. "Most of the time, in many studies, the whole is better than the sum of its parts", she says.

Assignments

1. Look up the unfamiliar words.
2. Translate the above paragraph into Korean.
3. Memorize the useful expressions.

27 Exclusive list

I have some concerns about the guest list for my daughter's upcoming **nuptials**. She has always been budget conscious, and I appreciate her attempts to keep the guest list to a minimum, but it's created a problem.

She and her fiance initially decided to limit the guests to those 18 and older. Unfortunately, this would have **excluded** her first cousins, plus some of her fiance's close family. I suggested setting the age at 12 and above, thinking his would **appease** all family members and we wouldn't have to worry about little ones disrupting the ceremony or disrupting the ceremony or distracting their parents. However, this resulted in a sizable disagreement, and she now has decided to include all children.

I would like to share this wonderful event with my extended family and included my aunts, uncles and first cousins on my portion of the guest list. My daughter revised the list to exclude my uncle and most of my cousins. She says she is close to only one of my cousins and **eliminate**d the rest. I explained that it is inappropriate to include one cousins and not the others, just as it is wrong to invite my father's sister, but not his brother.

These disagreement are causing a great deal of unhappiness, and I don't know how to keep the peace for everyone. please help settle this. -Distraught Mother

Who is paying for the wedding? If it is your daughter and her fiance, they get to determine how many guests. They can, however give you a specific number of invitations, allowing you to make the necessary decisions about your relatives. We agree that, barring a feud, she should invite both her great-aunt and great-uncle, but the bride's mother's first cousins are a different story. If she is close to only one, she does not need to invite the others. If you want them to attend the festivities, perhaps you could offer to pay the excess costs involved.

Assignments

1. Look up the unfamiliar words.
2. Translate the above paragraph into Korean.
3. Memorize the useful expressions.

28 Why French Fries Are Such Good Comfort Food

Ever wonder why French fries, potato chips and Cheetos are so **appealing** when you're feeling stressed? A new study suggests that elevated levels of salt in the body lower stress hormones and raise levels of oxytocin, a hormone involved in love and other social connections. The research, which was conducted in rats, was published in the Journal of Neuroscience. It found that rats' response to a stressful situation — being tied down — depended on how much salt they had in their bodies. When restrained, rats with high salt levels showed less activity in their brain's stress systems, compared with rats with normal salt levels.

Having high salt levels is technically called **hypernatremia** (geeky fact : the word suggests high levels of NA, the chemical abbreviation for the element sodium, which is an important part of salt), and rats in this state also recovered faster from being stressed.

Moreover, the hypernatremic rats had elevated levels of **oxytocin** — a compound known as the "love hormone" for its role in helping to create social bonds, between friends, lovers or parents and children. Oxytocin is crucial to the processes that allow love and social contact to reduce stress. Not surprisingly, rats with lots of oxytocin showed less anxiety in social interactions. (The effects of oxytocin are complicated, however — it doesn't always produce love and trust — but it is a significant player in those emotions.

Bartenders often provide salty snacks to **capitalize on** what having hypernatremia is most likely to make you feel : thirst. And indeed, drinking behavior may provide a clue as to why salt may be stress-relieving.

"We're calling this the Watering Hole Effect", said lead author Eric Krause, an assistant professor of psychiatry at the University of Cincinnati, in a press release. "When you're thirsty, you have to overcome some amount of fear and anxiety to approach a **communal** water source. And you want to facilitate those interactions — that way everyone can get to the water source."

No matter what they happen to be serving...

Assignments

1. Look up the unfamiliar words.
2. Translate the above paragraph into Korean.
3. Memorize the useful expressions.

29 Study : Having a Bad Job Is Worse than No Job For Mental Health

Maybe unemployment isn't so bad after all. A new study says that, income **notwithstanding**, having a demanding, unstable and thankless job may make you even unhappier than not having a job at all.

Given that a paid position gives workers purpose and a structured role, researchers had long thought that having any job would make a person happier than being unemployed. That turns out to be true if you move into a high-quality job — but taking a bad job is **detrimental** to mental health.

Australian National University researchers looked at how various **psychosocial** work attributes affect well-being. They found that poor-quality jobs — those with high demands, low control over decision making, high job insecurity and an effort-reward imbalance — had more adverse effects on mental health than joblessness.

The researchers analyzed seven years of data from more than 7,000 respondents of an Australian labor survey for their Occupational and Environmental Medicine study in which they wrote :

As hypothesized, we found that those respondents who were unemployed had significantly poorer mental health than those who were employed. However, the mental health of those who were unemployed was comparable or more often superior to those in jobs of the poorest psychosocial quality.

The current results therefore suggest that employment strategies seeking to promote positive outcomes for unemployed individuals need to also take account of job design and workplace policy.

Moving from unemployment to a job with high psychosocial quality was associated with improvements in mental health, the authors said. Meanwhile, the mental health of people in the least-satisfying jobs declined the most over time — and the worse the job, the more it affected workers' well-being.

Unemployed people in the Australian study had a mental-health score (based on the five-item Mental Health Inventory, which measures depression, anxiety and positive well-being in the previous month) of 68.5. Employed people had an average score of 75.1. The researchers found that moving from unemployment to a good job raised workers' scores by 3.3 points, but taking a bad job led to a 5.6-point drop below average. That was worse than remaining unemployed, which led to decline of about one point.

These findings underscore the importance of employment to a person's well-being. Rather than seeking any new job, the study suggests, people who are unemployed or stuck doing **lousy** work should seek new positions that offer more security, autonomy and a reasonable workload. But that's a lot easier said than done.

Perhaps employers could be persuaded to be more mindful of the mental health of their workers — happier employees are a benefit to their employers. "The **erosion** of work conditions", the researchers noted, "may incur a health cost, which over the longer term will be both economically and socially counter-productive."

Assignments

1. Look up the unfamiliar words.
2. Translate the above paragraph into Korean.
3. Memorize the useful expressions.

30 Feel like a slave

My parents owns a restaurant. I am employed there, but am looking for a new job. Why? Because I feel like a slave. I was hired as a server. But I have to go to work early to start off as a hostess, then hit the floor as a server, and finish off with bussing tables and closing out the **till**. I show up early when others call in sick, and often stay late to make sure everything is done right. Yet my dad complains that I'm "milking them for all they're worth" because I expect to be paid. If I say anything about it to my mother, she brushes it off. My parents expect me to become the manager someday, but I have told them repeatedly that I do not want the position.

None of my co-workers respects me, and they assume I get away with stuff because I'm the bosses' daughter. I have worked 11-hour shifts when no one else will come in. I have worked eight days in a row to cover someone else's shift, but no one will cover mine. I take no vacations.

How do I continue to handle this stress until I find a new job? -Frustrated

Your parents are **groom**ing you to someday take over the restaurant and need you to understand that the boss has the responsibility to work harder than everyone else. If you do not intend to follow them into the business, you should inform them immediately, suggest they hired a real manager, insist on being paid and treated as a regular server, and spend more time looking for another job.

Assignments

1. Look up the unfamiliar words.
2. Translate the above paragraph into Korean.
3. Memorize the useful expressions.

31 Friends with benefits

My husband and I have been married 22 years and have two children. "Myles" works for a large company known for its long workweeks. He and a woman, "Lara", co-manage the organization. Myles has always liked Lara and respects their working relationships. I never suspected a thing until they went on a business trip to Europe last fall.

Although there were other co-workers present, the only pictures Myles had were of Lara. Worse, she apparently "borrowed" his camera and took a photo of a friend's half-naked breasts. She sent me an e-mail apologizing, claiming she'd had too much to drink. Myles has increased the time he spends with Lara and decreased his time with me.

He ignored my request to attend our daughter's soccer game in order to have drinks with Lara. He took her out for her birthday at "our" special restaurant. When we took a family vacation, he bought gifts for her. I accused him of having an emotional affair and he denied it. He says Lara is just a good friend. Well, I am increasingly uncomfortable with this friendship. Myles insists that since he tells me about their time together, it is safe for me to accept this special relationship.

What can I do? -Worried and Unsure

Myles is playing a dangerous game. Even if he is not cheating, it wouldn't take much to step over that line.

His "honesty" is a **manipulative** way of getting your permission to continue while he denies his true feelings. You both need to sit down with a counselor and get professional guidance before it's too late.

Assignments

1. Look up the unfamiliar words.
2. Translate the above paragraph into Korean.
3. Memorize the useful expressions.

32 In her shadow

I have been best friends with "Claire" since junior high. She is **nothing short of** a knockout, with a sweet personality to match. We have always been very close, and I treasure our friendship.

The problem is, when we are out together, men are interested in Claire but feel she is unapproachable because she is so beautiful. Instead, they talk me up to try to get their foot in the door with her. Quite frankly, I am fed up with men only talking to me because they know I am friends with Claire. Then, when she isn't interested in them, I have to let them down. It's exhausting.

I am successful, educated, smart and funny, and I'm not bad looking, either, but men are only interested in my hot friend. This has been going on since high school, and I'm 35, for heaven's sake. How do I break this cycle or, at the very least, tactfully tell these men that I am not the key to Claire's heart? -Invisible

You are always going to suffer by comparison to Claire, so we strongly urge you not to try to meet men when you are with her. Her bright light makes everything else seem dim. On other occasions, when you are in Claire's company, it is perfectly OK to refuse to **intercede**. If you are approached about Claire, simply say, "Sorry, but if you are interested in my friend, you'll have to talk to her directly."

Assignments

1. Look up the unfamiliar words.
2. Translate the above paragraph into Korean.
3. Memorize the useful expressions.

33 New Parents

What can you do to relieve your tension when the baby cries **incessantly**? There are specific ways to get through this time, and they're important to learn. With extreme frustration, the temptation is to grab and shake the baby-which can result in permanent brain damage.

Don't get to this point. Have a plan ready to help take care of yourself.

The first step is to let go of assigning fault in the situation.

"Don't blame the baby — she can't help it", says Katherine Gordy Levine, a psychotherapist and author of Parents are People Too (Penguin Books, 1997). "Don't blame yourself. You are doing the best you can."

Levine, who has advised parents and been a **foster** parent, offers specific ideas :

- Sleep when you can. "Priorities at this stage should be feeding yourself, feeding your baby, changing her, and sleeping", she says.

- Use self-soothing exercises, such as deep breathing and visualization.

- Arrange for time away from the baby. Hire a sitter, exchange babysitting, or call helpful relatives and trusted friends to **babysit**.

- When you are alone with baby and cannot comfort her, put her in her **crib**, make sure she is safe, and without leaving the house, get away from the screaming. Play comforting music or take a shower.

- If you're in a new place or can't reach your helpers and feel you're going to become **abusive**, call or go to a neighborhood church or **synagogue** for help.

- Use a slogan to help you get them through these times. "My all-time favorite is 'Now is not forever,'"

Assignments

1. Look up the unfamiliar words.
2. Translate the above paragraph into Korean.
3. Memorize the useful expressions.

34 Help Your Kids Stay Safe While Surfing On-Line

Children should never give out their full name, address, phone number, or where they attend school to anyone they do not know without a parent's permission. **Remind** your children everything about them is their private information.

Explain to your children why it is important not to **volunteer** information to any company or individual.

Warn children that even reputable-looking web sites might not be what they appear to be, nor as friendly as they appear to be. Explain that someone might not be who he says he is online. Teach your children how to be **web-savvy**.

Offer to be with your child when he or she is online.

Investigate software tools that restrict sensitive personal information from being transmitted online, and tools that screen out material you don't want your children to see.

Assignments

1. Look up the unfamiliar words.
2. Translate the above paragraph into Korean.
3. Memorize the useful expressions.

35 Signs of Physical Abuse

Physical Indicators :

- Unexplained bruises and **welts** on the face, throat, upper arms, buttocks, thighs or lower back in unusual patterns or shapes which suggests the use of an instrument (belt buckle, electric cord) on an infant in various stages of healing that are seen after absences, weekends, or vacations.

- Unexplained burns, cigarette burns, especially burns found on palms, soles of feet, abdomen, buttocks; immersion burns producing "stocking" or "glove" marks on hands and feet; "doughnut shaped" on buttocks or genital area.

- **Rope burns.**

- Infected burns indicating delay in treatment; burns in the shape of common household utensils or appliances. Behavioral Indicators :

Assignments

1. Look up the unfamiliar words.
2. Translate the above paragraph into Korean.
3. Memorize the useful expressions.

36 U.S. DOT Proposes Rear View Visibility Rule to Protect Kids and the Elderly

The U.S. Department of Transportation today proposed a new safety regulation to help eliminate blind zones behind vehicles that can hide the presence of pedestrians, especially young children and the elderly. The proposed rule was required by Congress as part of the Cameron Gulbransen Kids Transportation Safety Act of 2007. Two-year old Cameron Gulbransen, for whom the Act is named, was killed when his father accidentally backed over him in the family's driveway.

"There is no more tragic accident than for a parent or **caregiver** to back out of a garage or driveway and kill or injure an undetected child playing behind the vehicle", said Transportation Secretary Ray LaHood. "The changes we are proposing today will help drivers see into those blind zones directly behind vehicles to make sure it is safe to back up."

The proposal, issued by the National Highway Traffic Safety Administration (NHTSA), would expand the required field of view for all passenger cars, pickup trucks, minivans, buses and low-speed vehicles with a gross vehicle weight rating of up to 10,000 pounds so that drivers can see directly behind the vehicle when the vehicle's transmission is in reverse. NHTSA believes automobile manufacturers will install rear mounted video cameras and in-vehicle displays to meet the proposed standards. To meet the requirements of the proposed rule, ten percent of new vehicles must comply by Sept. 2012, 40 percent by Sept. 2013 and 100 percent by Sept. 2014.

"The steps we are taking today will help reduce back-over fatalities and injuries not only to children, but to the elderly, and other pedestrians", said NHTSA Administrator David Strickland. "And while these changes will make a difference, drivers must remember that no technology can, or should, replace full attention and vigilance when backing up. Always know where your children are before you start your car and make sure you check that there is no one behind you before you back up."

NHTSA **estimate**s that, on average, 292 fatalities and 18,000 injuries occur each year as a result of back-over crashes involving all vehicles. Of these, 228 fatalities involve light vehicles weighing 10,000 pounds or less. Two particularly vulnerable populations — children and the elderly — are affected most. Approximately 44 percent of fatalities involving light vehicles are children under five — an unusually high percentage for any particular type of crash. In addition, 33 percent of fatalities involving light vehicles are elderly people 70 years of age or older.

Assignments

1. Look up the unfamiliar words.
2. Translate the above paragraph into Korean.
3. Memorize the useful expressions.

37 Pedestrian and Bicycle Safety

Each State should have **centralize**d program planning, implementation, and coordination to promote pedestrian and bicycle safety program issues as part of a comprehensive highway safety program. Evaluation should be used to revise existing programs, develop new programs, and determine progress and success of pedestrian and bicycle safety programs. The State Highway Safety Office should :

- Train program staff to effectively **coordinate** the implementation of recommended activities;

- Provide leadership, training, and technical assistance to other State agencies and local pedestrian and bicycle safety programs and projects;

- Conduct regular problem identification and evaluation activities to determine pedestrian and bicyclist **fatality**, injury, and crash trends and to provide guidance in development and implementation of countermeasures;

- Promote proper and legal riding practices and the proper

use of bicycle helmets as a primary measures to reduce death and injury among bicyclists;

- Coordinate with the State Department of Transportation to ensure provision of a safe environment for pedestrians and bicyclists through engineering measures such as sidewalks and bicycle facilities in the planning and design of all highway projects;

- Support the **enforcement** by local enforcement agencies of State laws affecting pedestrians and bicyclists; and

- Develop safety **initiatives** to reduce fatalities and injuries among high-risk groups as indicated by crash and injury data trends, including children, older adults, and alcohol-impaired pedestrians and bicyclists.

Assignments

1. Look up the unfamiliar words.
2. Translate the above paragraph into Korean.
3. Memorize the useful expressions.

부 록

Various Reading Vocabulary

부록 Various Reading Vocabulary

01. Suggestions from the Child Welfare League of America

vulnerable	취약한, 연약한
playgroup	놀이학교
time-out	중간휴식
abuse	오용, 남용, 학대 child abuse 아동학대
nurture	양육하다, 양성하다, 마음속으로 키우다
respite care	일시적 위탁, 간호
constitute	~을 구성하다
berate	질책하다
hygiene	위생

02. Introduction – What is Tourism?

mode	방법, 방식, 형태
domesticated	길든, 가정적인
stabilize	안정시키다, 안정되다
revenue	정부·기관의 수익
employer	고용주, 고용인

03. Our sweet home

behavior	행동, 행실
hypocrite	위선자
stand up for	~을 옹호하다
authority	권위
demand	요구하다
properly	제대로, 적절히
tough spot	곤란한 입장
on the same page	합심한
back up	~을 도와주다

04. Why Having Kids Is Bad for Your Health

knock	타격
parenthood	부모임
array	집합체, 배열
body mass index	신체용적지수
chug	(음료수)를 단숨에 마시다
saturated	포화된
doppelganger	도플갱어
relentless	끈질긴
fuss with	안달하다, 호들갑 떨다
coax	구슬리다, 달래다
trade-off	균형
pediatrics	소아과
leftover	남은음식
nugget	작고 동그랗게 만든 것

undo	무효로 만들다, 원상태로 돌리다
intervene	개입하다
perpetuate	영구화하다
corn dog	콘도그
coerce	강압하다
set the table	식탁을 차리다
prep work	준비작업
elliptical	함축된, 타원형의

05. Shutting him away

stroke	(뇌졸중)발작
homebody	집에 있기를 좋아하는 사람
care facility	요양시설
reluctantly	마지못해서, 꺼려하여
heartbroken	비통해 하는

06. Husband who lied

paperwork	서류 작업, 문서 업무
amicable	우호적인, 원만한
enrage	격분하게 하다
shambles	난장판, 어수선한 상태
annul	취소하다, 무효하게 하다

07. Inconsiderate hubbie

disgusted	넌덜머리 나는

08. Mommy trouble

disrespectful	무례한
bickering	말다툼, 언쟁
cry to	~에게 울며 매달리다
badmouth	안 좋게 말하다
convincing	설득력 있는, 확실한

09. Filthy friend

filthy	아주 더러운, 추잡한
vacuum	진공청소를 하다
countertop	조리대, 동의어 worktop

10. Stressed out? Wondering what to do?

challenging	도전적인
encourage	격려하다
recognize	인식하다

11. More than blood ties

regret	후회하다
family gathering	가족모임
obituary	사망기사, 부고
have the nerve to	~할 용기가 있다
inclusive	폭넓은, 포괄적인

12. Caught in the middle

compliment	칭찬
disconnection	단절
pick sides	편을 짜다
have an elephant on one's shoulder	마음이 무겁다
advocate	지지하다, 옹호하다, 지지자

13. Accused husband

compensate	보상하다, 보상금을 주다
disagree	의견이 다르다

14. Fashion that satisfies everyone

midriff	(배와 가슴 사이의)몸통
low-rise	낮은
offensive	모욕적인, 불쾌한
preteen	사춘기 직전의 아이
mature	성숙한
preach	설교하다
patronize	후원하다, 애용하다

15. Easy Disciplining

cry out	비명을 지르다
out of fashion	한물 간
cranky	까다로운, 기이한
get away with	~을 모면하다, 하고 싶은 대로 하다

alter	바꾸다
squall	비명을 지르다
get away with murder	자기 하고싶은 대로 다하다
spank	찰싹 때리다
enforce	집행하다, 실시하다
consistent	한결같은, 일관된

16. Tobacco-Free Kids

preventable	예방 가능한
exempt	면제되는
aggressive	공격적인
addiction	중독

17. Cradle robber

approve of	찬성하다, 괜찮다고 생각하다
tighten up	더 엄격해지다
suspend	연기하다, 중단하다
flirt with	추파를 던지다
levelheaded	온건한, 신중한
comparison shopping	경쟁상품 비교

18. Her cheatin' heart

alley	골목, 좁은 길
defensive	방어적인
shady	수상한 구석이 있는

snoop	기웃거리다, 염탐하다, 염탐꾼, 염탐
recommend	추천하다
transparent	투명한

19. For the sake of our baby

attack	공격하다
decide	결심하다
well-behaved	행실이 단정한
accomplish	성취하다

20. Not Daddy's girl

rage	격노
snarl	으르렁거리다

grit one's teeth

If you grit your teeth, you press your upper and lower teeth tightly together, usually because you are angry about something.

out of proportion	균형이 안 맞는, 안 어울리는
put a lid on	~을 억제하다

21. Big age gap

blessing	축복
biological children	친자

22. Hooked on Addiction : From Food to Drugs to Internet Porn

neuroscience	신경과학
obscenity	외설, 음란
prosecution	기소, 고발
opioids	합성 진통제 · 마취제
subvert	전복시키다
homeostasis	항상성
bizarre	기이한
circular reasoning	순환론
pathway	좁은 길, 오솔길, 경로
sabotage	사보타주, 방해행위
compulsive	강박적인, 조절이 힘든
psychiatry	정신의학
craving	열망, 갈망
full-fledged	제대로 자격을 갖춘
relapse	재발
blurry	모호한
pathological	병적인, 병의
unaffordable	too expensive to be afforded
blow off	빼먹다

23. When Mom Exercises in Pregnancy, Her Baby's Heart Benefits

plausible	타당할 것 같은
indulge	마음껏 하다
regimen	식이요법
upend	뒤집다

mindset	사고방식, 태도
morph	변하다
guilt	죄책감
trimester	임신 3개월
anatomist	해부학자
noninvasive	확장하지 않은
fetal	태아의
cardiac	심장의
attrition	소모
be slated for	~하기로 되어 있다

24. Can't Get Enough Coffee? It Might Be in Your Genes

sludgy	질벅질벅한
descent	혈통, 가문
variant	변종, 이형
chromosomes	염색체
mutation	돌연변이, 변화
contribute to	기여하다
toxic	유독성의
predispose	~하게 만들다, 취약하게 하다

25. Why Exercise Won't Make You Thin

cardio	심장 강화운동
towering	우뚝 솟은, 대단히 뛰어난
wedge	쐐기
contraption	기계장치
expiation	속죄, 보상
gastronomical	미식의
grimly	잔인하게, 엄하게
gut	내장, 배
obesity	비만, 비대
shed	흘리다, 내뿜게 하다
negate	무효화하다
accrue	누적되다

26. An Apple a Day Keeps Cholesterol at Bay?

keep ~ at bay	저지하다
credence	신빙성, 믿음
adage	속담, 격언
inflammation	염증

27. Exclusive list

nuptials	결혼식
exclude	배제시키다
appease	요구를 들어주다, 달래다
eliminate	제거하다

28. Why French Fries Are Such Good Comfort Food

appealing	매력적인
hypernatremia	고나트륨혈증
oxytocin	옥시토신
capitalize on	~을 활용하다, 기회로 삼다
communal	공동의

29. Study : Having a Bad Job Is Worse than No Job For Mental Health

notwithstanding	~에도 불구하고
detrimental	해로운
psychosocial	심리사회적인
lousy	안 좋은, 엉망인
erosion	부식, 침식, 짓무름

30. Feel like a slave

till	돈 서랍
groom	대비시키다, 훈련시키다

31. Friends with benefits

manipulative	조작의
permission	허락, 허가

32. In her shadow

nothing short of	아주 ~한
knockout	엄청 멋진 사람
intercede	탄원하다

33. New Parents

incessantly	쉴 새 없이
foster	양…
babysit	애를 보다
crib	거처, 집
abusive	모욕적인, 폭력적인
synagogue	유대교 회당

34. Help Your Kids Stay Safe While Surfing On-Line

Remind	상기시키다
volunteer	자진해서 말하다
web-savvy	웹 상식, 웹 지식

35. Signs of Physical Abuse

welts	부은 자국

rope burns abrasion (usually on the hands) caused by friction from a rope

36. U.S. DOT Proposes Rear View Visibility Rule to Protect Kids and the Elderly

caregiver	돌보는 사람
estimate	평가하다, 추정하다

37. Pedestrian and Bicycle Safety

centralize	중앙집권화 하다
coordinate	편성하다
fatality	사망자
enforcement	강화
initiatives	계획

References

문영수 · 천재윤(2005). 누워서 보는 영어, 백산출판사.

문영수 · 천재윤(2005). 크게 웃고 가는 리딩스킬, 백산출판사.

문영수 · 천재윤(2010). Grammar Free Zone, 백산출판사.

문영수 · 천재윤(2011). Survival Tourism English, 백산출판사.

천재윤(2006). 술술 내려 읽는 미국영어, 백산출판사.

사전

Collins COBUID Advanced Learner's English Dictionary(2006), Harpercollins Publishers

Internet site

http://www.childabuse.org/

http://www.time.com/time/

http://www.creators.com/

저자약력

문영수(文榮秀)

전북대학교 인문대 영어영문학과 졸업
고려대학교 대학원 영어영문학과 졸업(문학석사)
전북대학교 대학원 영어영문학과 졸업(문학박사)
광신대학교 신학대학원 졸업(목회학 석사)
총회신학원 수료
전북대학교 인문대 강사 역임
University of Wisconsin(Madison) 객원교수
현) 호원대학교 관광대학 호텔관광학부 교수
 무디교회 담임목사

주요저서

ABC 대학기초영어(학문출판사, 1999)
Pops English Conversation(학문출판사, 2002)
누워서 보는 영어(백산출판사, 2005)
크게 웃고 가는 리딩스킬(백산출판사, 2005)
Grammar Free Zone(백산출판사, 2010)
Survival Tourism English(백산출판사, 2011)
Contemporary Survival English(백산출판사, 2011) 外

주요논문

우울증의 목회 상담적 치유 연구(2009)
시대를 향한 한 시인의 노력: 브라우닝의 낙관주의 연구(2008) 外

천재윤(千才銃)

Major/ Sociolinguistics
University of Hawaii NICE course(full scholarship)
Chonbuk National University Graduate School(full scholarship)
전) With Me English Academy Representative
 Dr. Cheon's English Academy Representative
현) Win Language Academy Representative
 Chonbuk National Univ./ Howon Univ. Visiting Prof.

주요저서

누워서 보는 영어(백산출판사, 2005)
크게 웃고 가는 리딩스킬(백산출판사, 2005)
술술 내려 읽는 미국영어(백산출판사, 2006)
Grammar Free Zone(백산출판사, 2010)
Survival Tourism English(백산출판사, 2011)
Contemporary Survival English(백산출판사, 2011) 外

주요논문

A Sociolinguistic Study on the Speech Act of 'Gomapseupnida' in Korean(2010) 外

Contemporary Survival English

2011년 6월 25일 초판 1쇄 인쇄
2011년 6월 30일 초판 1쇄 발행

저 자 문 영 수 · 천 재 윤

발행인 (寅製) 진 욱 상

발행처 백산출판사

서울시 성북구 정릉3동 653-40
등록 : 1974. 1. 9. 제 1-72호
전화 : 914-1621, 917-6240
FAX : 912-4438
http://www.ibaeksan.kr
editbsp@naver.com

값 12,000원
ISBN 978-89-6183-478-0